A Cognitive-Behavioral Perspective
on
Problematic Alcohol and Other Drug Use

By
Russ Fry

Vita

Russ Fry lives in Burlington, Iowa. He received a Bachelor of Arts in History at the University of Northern Iowa. He has a Masters of Arts in Social Studies from Excelsior College in Albany, New York, with an emphasis in History, Psychology, and Sociology. This book is his thesis. Russ is a retired Community Treatment Coordinator for Iowa Community Corrections. He specialized in cognitive-behavioral interventions for Precontemplative and Contemplative offenders. Russ conducted educational/motivational enhancement programs for offenders who were at high risk for re-offending because of alcohol and other drug use.

Abstract

This paper describes a model of alcohol and other drug use as a continuum with extremely problematic behavior on one end and non-problematic behavior on the other. A drinker or drug user's place on the continuum and the character of their drinking or using behavior (including motivations to use, problems that can result from using and resistance to change) depends on the number, magnitudes and variety of the biological, psychological and sociological factors that contribute to their perception of the rewards over costs.

Problematic alcohol and drug use is described in a cognitive-behavioral psychology that addresses cross-personal differences in innate responses to alcohol and other drugs, self/other nature of defining problematic behavior, self-defeating beliefs, the negative consequences of using neutralizing beliefs and the automatic/deliberate nature of human information processing and decision-making. It also deals with effective and ineffective methods for dealing with reduced efficacy. Cravings are described from a cognitive-behavioral perspective, as are the methods for managing them.

Table of Contents

I. INTRODUCTION
A. Problems Caused by Alcohol and Other Drugs

Remember that we deal with alcohol – cunning, baffling, powerful!

Alcoholics Anonymous

All "things" – from the tiniest virus to the greatest galaxy – are,
in reality, not things at all, but processes.

Future Shock
Alvin Toffler

In the movie *Leaving Las Vegas* the characters played by Nicholas Cage and Eliz-

abeth Shue go out for a night of drinking and gambling. Late into the evening, something

upsets Cage's character. He tips over a card table and knocks down a waitress. Just as the

security people grab him, the scene cuts to Cage sleeping on a sofa. He awakes with a

jolt. His whole body is shaking as he grabs for a bottle of liquor. As he tips it towards his

mouth, he discovers that it is empty. The scene then cuts to him kneeling on the floor in

front of an open refrigerator. He struggles to open the cap on a fresh bottle of alcohol. His

face looks pale and pasty. He is shaking so badly that he can barely pour the alcohol into

a carton of orange juice. His face is sweating and his hands trembling as he drinks down

his mixture. The scene next cuts to him having the dry heaves in the sink. As the alcohol

has its effect, he stops shaking and he shuffles off to bed with Shue's character. He asks

her how she managed to keep the security people from throwing him out of the casino

into the street. She replies that she told them he was an alcoholic.

Few people would disagree with her diagnosis. Fewer still would question that al-

cohol and other drug use causes a great many problems - such as: marital, family, self-

esteem, social ostracism, financial, employment, legal, and mental and emotional health.

Alcohol and other drugs can also damage a person's liver, heart, nervous system and

1

many other aspects of their physical health. Some people have mild problems in these areas, other have serious problems.

A dramatic example of a serious problem area caused by alcohol is that in any eight week period there are more people killed in alcohol related traffic crashes in the United States than there were people killed by terrorist, world wide, during the whole decade of the nineteen-nineties (Myers, 2002).

B. Dichotomous View

"Alcoholism" and "drug addiction" as viewed by the 12-Step Tradition of Alcoholics Anonymous is considered a disease, actually two diseases (2001). It is a disease of the body and a disease of the mind. Every time an "alcoholic" takes a drink, a craving for more alcohol begins and the "alcoholic" will not be able to stop drinking until they are intoxicated. This, AA says, can never be changed. An "alcoholic's" body will never allow them to drink safely.

Alcoholics Anonymous also believes that "alcoholism" is a disease of the mind. An "alcoholic," not in remission, cannot resist taking that first drink. The disease of the mind can be put into remission by turning one's will over to their higher power. The spiritual awakening that comes from this returns them to sanity and gives them the ability to not take that first drink. Many in the 12-Step Tradition believe that this is the only path to remission for "true alcoholics" and that death or insanity awaits those of them who do not stop drinking.

On the other hand, the American Psychiatric Association does not recognize "alcoholism," per se, as a disorder. Instead, they classify problematic use as being either a "substance abuse disorder" or a "substance dependent disorder." It defines Substance

Abuse as (APA, 1994, pp.182-183):

> A. a maladaptive pattern of substance use leading to clinically significant impairment or distress, as manifested by one (or more) of the following, occurring within a 12-month period:
>
> 1. recurrent substance use resulting in a failure to fulfill major role obligations at work, school, or home (e.g., repeated absences or poor work performance related to substance use; substance-related absences, suspensions, or expulsions from school; neglect of children or household)
>
> 2. recurrent substance use in situations in which it is physically hazardous (e.g., driving an automobile or operating a machine when impaired by substance use)
>
> 3. recurrent substance-related legal problems (e.g., arrests for substance-related disorderly conduct)
>
> 4. continued substance use despite having persistent or recurrent social or interpersonal problems caused or exacerbated by the effects of the substance (e.g., arguments with spouse about consequences of intoxication, physical fights)
>
> B. the symptoms have never met the criteria for Substance Dependence for this class of substance.

They define Substance Dependence as a maladaptive pattern of substance use,

leading to clinically significant impairment or distress, as manifested by three (or more)

of the following, occurring at any time in the same 12-month period (APA, 1994, p. 181):

> 1. tolerance, as defined by either of the following:
>   a. a need for markedly increased amounts of the substance to achieve intoxication or desired effect
>   b. markedly diminished effect with continued use of the same amount of the substance
>
> 2. withdrawal, as manifested by either of the following:
>   a. the characteristic withdrawal syndrome for the substance
>   b. the same (or a closely related) substance is taken to relieve or avoid withdrawal symptoms
>
> 3. the substance is often taken in larger amounts or over a longer period than was intended
>
> 4. there is a persistent desire or unsuccessful efforts to cut down or control substance use
>
> 5. a great deal of time is spent in activities necessary to obtain the substance

(e.g., visiting multiple doctors or driving long distances), use the substance (e.g., chain-smoking), or recover from its effects

6. important social, occupational, or recreational activities are given up or reduced because of substance use

7. the substance use is continued despite knowledge of having a persistent or recurrent physical or psychological problem that is likely to have been caused or exacerbated by the substance (e.g., current cocaine use despite recognition of cocaine-induced depression, or continued drinking despite recognition that an ulcer was made worse by alcohol consumption).

C. Continuum View

While much suffering surrounds people who meet any of these definitions, many problems are caused by people who fall short of them. For example, half of all people arrested for drunk driving in the United States are not "alcohol abusers" or "alcohol dependent" (NHTSA, 1996). Another report from the National Highway Traffic Safety Administration says that, "even if all alcohol-related fatal crashes involving repeat offenders were eliminated, at least 90% of all fatal crashes would remain" (Jones and Lacy, 2000). Problematic behavior is caused by a variety of people with a variety of attractions to alcohol and other drugs. If society's perspective of problematic alcohol and drug use is too narrow and concerns itself with only those people exhibiting the strongest attractions, it will miss an opportunity to improve many other lives and make our communities a better place in which to live.

As will be developed and qualified in detail later, people attempt to maximize rewards and minimize costs. Rewards and costs are determined by the factors contributed by a person's biological make up, their psychological states and their sociological circumstances. The number of life situations that provide rewards or extract costs varies among individuals. Therefore, some people may find drinking and other drug using rewarding in

4

more situations than others do. The more drinking or using situations a person finds rewarding, the more attractive drinking and using becomes.

Since the rewards and costs for drinking and using are determined by biopsychosocial factors that vary among individuals, the magnitudes of a particular reward or cost will also vary among individuals. Some people, for example, the pharmacological effects of drinking or using make them feel very good, while others can take it or leave it. Shy people might feel more confident after a few drinks. Others may need to drink in order to feel confident in social situations. Depending on a person's culture, drinking (and even drug using) may be considered acceptable in certain social situations and not in others. The greater the magnitude of a person's overall rewards over costs for drinking or using, the greater is their attraction to it becomes.

Finally, the variety of reward types a person experiences in a situation will also affect the attractiveness of drinking and using. For example, some people drink or use for recreational and social reasons. Other people do not. Some people drink or use to escape dysphoria. Others do not. Some people drink or use to avoid withdrawal symptoms. For some, this is not a concern. The more reward types a person experiences, the more numerous the opportunities to experience multiple rewards in any single drinking and using situation becomes.

The greater a person's overall attraction to alcohol and other drugs, the more likely they are to drink or use, the more frequently they are likely to do so and more likely in greater quantities. A person who is highly attracted to drinking or using will experience more ambivalence and be more resistive to change if their drinking or using becomes a problem. Problems for such people are more likely to remain unresolved and become exasperated.

The model presented herein holds that the use of alcohol and other drugs falls on a continuum with extremely problematic behavior on one end and non-problematic behavior on the other. A user's place on the continuum and the character of their drinking or other drug using behavior (including motivations to use, problems that can result from drinking or other drug using and resistance to change) depends on the number, magnitudes and variety of the biological, psychological and sociological factors that contribute to their perception of the rewards over costs of their drinking or other drug using behaviors.

If Alvin Toffler's quote at the beginning of this introduction is correct, that everything from viruses to galaxies are processes, we can understand why problematic alcohol and other drug use is seen as "baffling." People have a tendency to take a slice out of a process and call it a "thing." However, this does not explain that "thing," it only describes it. "Alcoholism" is a slice out of a process of how humans make decisions in general and decisions about using alcohol in particular. Alcoholics Anonymous does not explain "alcoholism," it only describes it.

In the same way, the DSM IV of the American Psychiatric Association does not explain substance abuse or substance dependency; it describes a syndrome by listing its signs and symptoms. The DSM IV is atheoretical and leaves explanations for disorders to the orientation of the various treatment providers who use it (McGuire and Troisi, 1998).

In their book *Darwinian Psychiatry*, Michael McGuire and Alfonso Troisi state that, " psychiatry operates without a theory that can explain both non-disordered and disordered states, that can organize and prioritize its findings, that can provide novel and testable hypothesis about causes of disorder, that can guide its research, and that can focus clinical interventions" (1998, p. ix).

To parallel these thoughts, there will not be an accurate understanding of the full range of problematic alcohol and other drug use until there is an adequate model that explains both non-problematic alcohol and other drug use and problematic use on a continuum. An explanation can only be derived by viewing a "thing" as part of the process in which it is embedded.

D. Cognitive-Behavioral Psychology

This model provides a cognitive-behavioral perspective on problematic alcohol and other drug use. It discusses the cross-personal differences in innate responses to alcohol and other drugs, self/other nature of defining problematic behavior, self-defeating beliefs, the negative consequences of using neutralizing beliefs and the automatic/deliberate nature of human information processing and decision-making. It also deals with effective and ineffective methods for dealing with reduced efficacy.

The work of Albert Ellis (1961, 1988, 1992) and Aaron Beck (1993) will provide the main perspective on the cognitive-behavioral psychology used herein. Albert Bandura's moral disengagement theory (1996) will explain how the use of neutralizing thoughts can erode a person's values in favor of drinking and using other drugs.

The work of Seymour Epstein (1993, 1994, 1998) will provide further structure to the cognitive-behavioral psychology with his concept of the automatic/deliberate nature of human information processing and decision-making.

In addition, humans are social creatures and do not function in a vacuum. No model of human behavior would be complete without exploring the affects of the social environment on behavior.

E. Biopsychosocial Perspective

This model also holds that the factors that contribute to a person's attraction to alcohol and other drug use are to be found in biology, psychology and the social environment (Pilgram, 2003). A medical analogy will clarify why this broad perspective is useful. A biological explanation of a heart attack might be that a person's heart muscles received an insufficient supply of blood, resulting in its inability to pump adequately and the subsequent death of some of the heart cells.

Why, though, might a person have an insufficient supply of blood to their heart muscles? One of the possibilities is that they had arterioscleroses, hardening of the arteries.

Arterioscleroses certainly has a biological explanation – cholesterol and fatty deposits build up on the lining of arteries in susceptible people and eventually block blood flow to heart muscles and other parts of the body. Where does the cholesterol and fat come from? Some people eat fatty and cholesterol-laden diets because the pleasurable taste sensations they provide temporarily sooth their troubled minds. This is not a biological cause, it is psychological. Some people eat fatty and cholesterol-laden diets because they were raised in a culture that traditionally eats fried foods. That is a sociological cause.

Which of these features caused the heart attack? That is the wrong question to ask. They all could contribute to the outcome. It is an individual's unique combination of their biological makeup, their psychological states and the social environment in which they learn and live that resulted in the heart attack. Again, different people and their problems have different contributing factors that cause differing consequences. Viewing behaviors, such as problematic alcohol and other drug use, in an undifferentiated way is self-limiting and misleading (Ewing, 1980).

F. Models

Science frequently uses models as aids to understanding complex systems (Gardner and Kemer, 1993). If asked, many people would describe an atom as "a miniature solar system" (Chester, 1978). This is called Rutherford's model and was formulated in the early nineteen hundreds. It became obsolete within a few years as new information became available. Yet, it remains popular today because it is easy to understand and satisfactorily explains many physical phenomena until some very subtle details are considered. Models help individuals understand the overall process of a complex system by focusing on the big picture. They are often used as tools from which deeper understandings can be discovered by providing an original framework from which to work.

A great deal of research has been carried out on alcohol and other drug use and much has been written on the subject. No single work could expect to cover it all in detail. However, models are not meant to be comprehensive explanations of a phenomenon.

Rather they are conceptual frameworks into which the known facts can be successfully placed and to serve as guides for searching for new information.

Models often contain research findings, clinical opinions and hypotheses. Not everything expressed in a model need be proven, at least initially, in order for it to be useful. However, models must be logical, internally consistent and not be inconsistent with the known facts.

While the ability to help people with their alcohol and other drug problems is one measure of a model's usefulness, treatment issues are not a point of discussion herein. However, an outline for change that is suggested by the model will be presented.

G. Terminology

"When I use a word," Humpty Dumpty said in a rather scornful voice, "it means just what I choose it to mean, nothing more nor less."
Through the Looking Glass and What Alice Found There
Lewis Carroll

What's in a name? That which we call a rose by any other name would smell as sweet.
William Shakespeare

Alcoholics Anonymous have their "alcoholics" and the American Psychiatric Association have their "substance abuse" and "substance dependent" disorders. Most models slice the process in different places and define their slices with their own terminology. Unfortunately, that adds much to the confusion surrounding problematic alcohol and drug use, as well as many other complex subjects. However, if a model provides a clear explanation of a phenomenon, its definitions will also provide a clear standard for a language to be used. Therefore, the terminology should be true to the model and not to current conventions. This does not mean that whatever is being labeled does not have to represent actual phenomena. To be an acceptable scientific model, all labels must be attached to measurable "things."

Herein alcohol and other drug use will be referred to as AOD. The discussion will be limited to intoxicating drugs - those that distort perceptions, alter moods and compromise judgment when taken in the range of quantities typically used (APA, 1994). This includes alcohol and most illegal drugs. Alcohol and other drug use that is problematic will be referred to as PAOD.

The model is broad enough to include non-intoxicating drugs and what have been called addictive behaviors, such as gambling. They are just special cases of problematic choices that arise from different contributing factors. However, they will not be included in the discussions.

The words "drinking" and "drinkers" refer respectively to the act of using AOD and people who use AOD. They can be used interchangeable with AOD, "using" and "users", as long as it is understood that alcohol and other drugs do not all share the same attributes. "Alcoholic" will be a term used to describe the subset of alcohol users as defined by Alcoholics Anonymous or as used in quotations. "Drug addict" or "addicts" are users as defined by the 12-Step Tradition as it applies to drugs or as used in quotations.

II. VALUES
A. Operant Conditioning

One of the key sets of principles that help explain human motivation and behavior is provided by the Behaviorist concept of operant conditioning (Benson, 2001). In their terms, an increase in a behavior that results from a rewarded is referred to as a positive reinforcement. An increase in a behavior that results from the avoidance of a cost is referred to as a negative reinforcement. Punishment refers to a decrease in a behavior because it incurs a cost.

Said another way, people tend to act in ways that they have found will lead to pleasure and that avoid pain. People seek out and do things that they have found will make them feel good or seek out and do things that will free them from things that they have found will make them feel bad.

While the complete mechanics are not yet known, alcohol and other drugs, such as marijuana, heroin and cocaine, create their pleasure producing effects by stimulating dopaminergic signal transmissions, which are part of the natural brain reward system (Chiara, 1997). Alcohol and other drugs act as chemical surrogates for natural rewards such as sex and food, but possibly more powerfully and persistently rewarding (Neuroscience Research and Medication Development, 1996).

B. Characteristics of Values

The concept of rewards and costs can be expanded in a general way to say that people value those things, objects or experiences, that they believe will make them feel good or that they believe will free them from things they do not like.

Things of value can be related to either physical or emotional pleasure. The pleasure may be either experienced immediately or delayed. The things of value might be concrete or abstract.

People also have personal concepts or beliefs about their self-image and of what it takes to be the "right kind" of person. They feel good when they live up to those standards and bad when they do not (Festinger, 1957; Ellis and Velten, 1992; Epstein and

Brodsky, 1993; Bandura, Barbaranelli, Caprara and Pastorelli, 1996). In a similar vein, they have beliefs about how things "should" be. They feel good when things are functioning "as they should" and bad when they are not (Ellis and Harper, 1961).

Though a person may value many things, each of them is not valued equally. They each carry different weights or magnitudes of value. The better a person expects something to make them feel, the stronger their attraction to it and the stronger their emotional urge to obtain it. The greater the expected bad feelings, the stronger their aversion and the stronger their emotional urge to avoid it.

C. Interpersonal Variations in Values

In addition to the differences in the magnitude of values for specific things, the specific things and the total number of things an individual value varies from person to person. One person might love one thing, while another person might hate it. Some people value many things. Others value fewer. The things a person values and the total number of things valued are dynamic, they vary over time.

There are wide variations between individuals, both in specific valued-things and in their magnitudes. How do these variations in kind and in degree come about? This is the age-old "nature verses nurture" debate. Most contemporary thinkers believe that variations, especially in behavior, can best be understood by describing how nature and nurture interact to produce a particular outcome (Moore, 2001). For example, tall people are tall in part because they inherited "tall people-making" genes from their parents. However, good nutrition, especially during critical developmental periods, inextricably affects the expression of genes and contributes to a person's overall height as well. Nevertheless, it is convenient to separate out the various factors in order to study their individual contributions.

There are scientific studies that support the idea that people can inherit a genetic predisposition that puts them at risk for PAOD. Studies that compare incidence of "alcoholism" among identical twins with fraternal twins show that identical twins share a similar history of "alcoholism" (or of not developing "alcoholism") more often than do fraternal twins (Genetics of Alcoholism, 1992; APA, 1994). This suggests a genetic or biological component to "alcoholism."

This conclusion is also supported by other studies that found that "alcoholism" among adoptees raised apart from their "alcoholic" birth parents was greater than among adoptees raised apart from their non-alcoholic birth parents (Genetics of Alcoholism, 1992; APA, 1994). Epidemiological studies estimate that between 40% and 60% of the risk of "alcoholism" and certain "drug addictions" is genetic (APA, 1994; Nestler, 2002).

For another example, a recent study by Mary Jeanne Keek, found that the brain releases a naturally occurring brain opiate called dynorphin that functions to restore homeostasis after cocaine has disturbed the brain's normal chemical balance (Nature's Own Antidote to Cocaine, 2002). It further found that some people carry a "high-output" version of the gene that develops the dynorphin producing mechanism, while some people carry a "low-output" version. For a "high-output" person, the effects of cocaine are dampened and they have a moderately pleasurable cocaine experience. On the other hand, a "low-output" person's cocaine use will be dampened less and subsequently they will have a more intense experience. The more intense the reward, the greater the attraction.

Genetic influences can also reduce alcohol use. People with the ALDH2 allele experience flushing of the skin, nausea and headaches after consuming alcohol (Alcohol and Minorities, 2002). These uncomfortable symptoms translate into two-thirds less alcohol consumption (Alcohol and Minorities, 2002) and reduced incidence of "alcohol abuse" and "dependency" (APA, 1994). An interesting point is that the ALDH2 allele occurs commonly in people of Asian heritage, but seldom in other racial groups.

These examples show that inherited biological interpersonal variations can result in different AOD experience for different people and different degrees of attraction to those experiences. It explains, in part, why some people will want to use over and over again, while other people can take it or leave it.

This does not, however, imply determinism (Ellis and Velten, 1992). Variations in the biologically induced rewards lead to variations in the attractiveness of the behavior that causes those rewards. A great attraction to something does not result in an inability to resist it. Rather, it just makes resisting it more difficult. Irresistible compulsions, as discussed later, are the result of different processes.

> Unless you are unlucky enough to have a rare and serious genetic
> condition, and most of us do not, the impact of genes upon our
> lives is a gradual, partial, blended sort of thing.
>
> *Genome*
> Matt Ridley

> The claim that personality is inherited has strong evidence behind
> it. But, at most, personality is only partly genetic. The degree of
> heritability hovers below .50 for all personality traits (except IQ,
> which may be around .75). Even by the most extreme estimates, at
> least half of personality is fixed. The other half of personality
> comes from what you do and from what happens to you – and this
> opens the door for therapy and self-improvement.
>
> *What You Can Change and What You Can't*
> Martin Seligman

An example of a psychological contribution to predispositions drink is the Reward Deficiency Syndrome (Blum, Cull, Braverman and Comings, 1996). It is also an example of interpersonal genetic variations as well. A genetic anomaly that was previously associated with "alcoholism" was also found with increased frequency among people with other compulsive, impulsive behaviors, such as substance abuse, smoking, obesity and pathological gambling. It is believed that some people have, to varying degrees, a "hard wired" sensory deprivation of the brain's reward mechanisms that interferes with their experiencing the normal rewards of everyday life. They suggest that this translates into stimulus-seeking behavior and encourages substance use because they release pleasure-causing dopamine in the brain.

The analysis of the social component of biopsychosocial models of PAOD lags behind the biological and psychological components (Wieczorek and Hanson, 1997). Nevertheless, environmental factors play an important role. People learn to value many of the things in their lives through their experience and how they were raised. People who grew up doing a variety of things for recreation are likely to turn out different from people who spent every evening playing in a corner of a bar while their parents drank. Children who were taught to problem solve often face life's difficulties more effectively than do children who saw their parents drink away their sorrows rather than trying to fix them.

Studies do show a link between PAOD and social factors. For example, there is a correlation between the commercial availability of alcohol and alcohol related traffic crashes (Alcohol and Minorities, 2002). Furthermore, there is a greater density of liquor stores in low-income and minority neighborhoods than in other neighborhoods and that this reflects an increase in alcohol problems in those areas (Alcohol and Minorities, 2002).

Inherited interpersonal biological variations, different psychological factors and different life experiences leave people with differing degrees of attractions to similar experience (Seligman, 1993; Moore, 2001). Some people may be strongly attracted to how AOD makes them feel. Other people will be only weakly attracted to their effects.

The things people value can be described as their wants, desires, hopes, dreams, ambitions, goals and purposes, to name a few. They are referred to, herein, as aspirations. Aspirations are all of those things that a person has in their lives that they aspire to keep, as well as those things that they do not now have, but aspire to have some day. They are the things, objects or experiences, that people value - the objectives of their goals.

The totality of the things a person values, in both number and respective weights, reflect the overall magnitude of their aspirations. Figure 1 is a graphic representation of the scale of magnitude of a person's overall aspiration. Some people's overall aspirations are high and are marked at the top of the scale. Other people have lower overall aspirations and are marked toward the bottom of the scale.

D. Cost/Reward Analysis

When a person perceives an opportunity to obtain one of their aspirations, they begin to weigh the costs verses the rewards of the opportunity (Andrews and Bonta, 1998; McGuire and Troisi, 1998). The expected costs are measured in terms of the things of value that they believe they will have to expend in order to acquire the expected rewards. If the combined magnitudes of the rewards outweighs the combined magnitudes of the costs, a person will likely decide that it is a good opportunity and act accordingly.

If the costs exceed the rewards, they will likely try another way of getting what they want or move on to some other goal (Andrews and Bonta, 1998).

A cost/reward analysis does not always take place with conscious deliberation and full consideration of the cost/rewards is not always made before a person acts. This point is an important one and will be developed later in the discussion of the automatic/deliberate nature of human information processing and decision-making.

FIGURE 1.

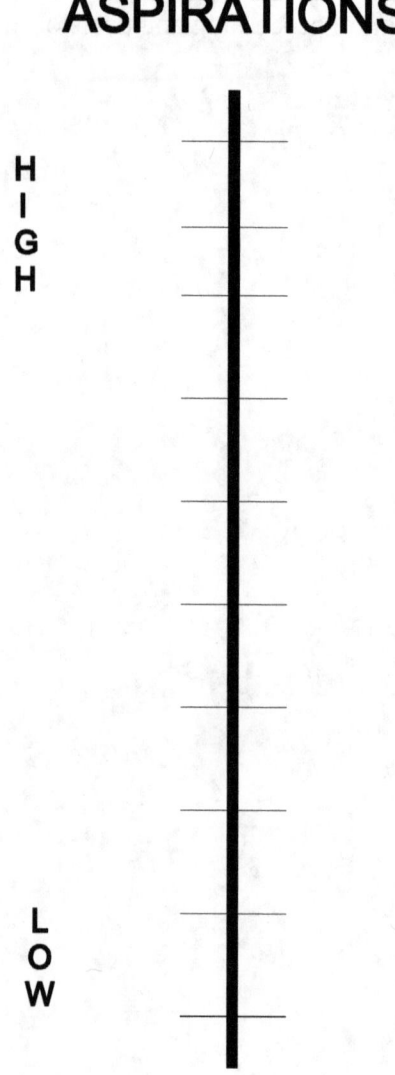

E. Values Systems

A person will have difficulties maximizing their aspirations if the system formed by their aspirations is not well-adjusted. A system of aspirations is not well-adjusted if some aspirations are unrealistic or if some are incongruent with the harmonious integration with the other aspirations. This will be true regardless of how intelligent or how competent a person might be. Wanting something that is impossible to obtain will obviously lead to failure. It is the lack of harmonious integration of aspirations that is more instructive to the causes of many problem situations.

If a person wants to two different things, but in obtaining one, the other is harmed, the person cannot maximize their aspirations. However, if their aspirations are well-adjusted, actions to obtain one either does not harm the others or may even support them in some way.

For example, a woman may have a good car and want to keep it. She enjoys it and would like to drive it all the time, but cannot drive during work hours. However, her job gives her money to maintain her car. Her car, in turn, helps her get to work. There is a mutually reciprocating trade-off between these aspirations that is harmonious and co-supporting.

A well-adjusted system of aspirations is stable and maximizing. A poorly adjusted system of aspirations, one in which one or more aspirations interferer with the attainment of other aspirations, is destabilizing and self-defeating. For example, a man may love to drink and love his job. However, if his drinking interferes with his job, he might be fired. Without a job, he has fewer means to obtain his alcohol and fulfill his other aspirations.

This is significant in regards to PAOD. It might be unrealistic for some people to aspire to drink like a "gentleman." Or, a man may aspire to experience the sense and ease of comfort that comes at once by taking a few drinks and also aspire to have a happy marriage. The two aspirations may be incongruent and impossible to maximize. A person in either of these situations will have problems until their circumstances are acknowledged and addressed.

III. REWARD TYPES
A. Recreational/Social Purposes

In addition to the number and magnitudes of rewarding drinking and using situations, the variety of reward types expressed in those situations will also contribute to a person's attraction to AOD. It is useful to group these reward types into categories or dimensions. This model groups them into: Recreational/Social Purposes, Palliative Psychological Relief and Escaping Withdrawal Effects. Classifying reward types this way not only helps explain why a person finds drinking attractive (or unattractive), but also provides a profile that directs the category-specific therapeutic strategies that will be needed to help a person trying to make changes.

People who use recreationally or for social purposes, do so because they believe that drinking makes it easier for them to have a good time (Ellis, McInerney, DiGiuseppe and Yeager, 1988). This is a positive reinforced reward. It creates pleasure.

People start drinking for the pharmacological pleasure, the exhilaration of getting high and to share the experience with others, as well as for the expectation that it will increase their abilities to successfully navigate their social environment (Beck, Wright, Newman and Liese, 1993).

Again, there are biological differences in how the person will react to a substance. The more pleasurable their pharmacological reaction, the more likely they are to use for these purposes. Along similar lines, the social setting in which the drinking takes place will affect a person's decisions. *Is it appropriate or not? What are the costs and rewards?* A psychological aspect might be, *I don't care about what other's think.*

B. Palliative Psychological Relief

When some people are feeling bad emotionally, they use alcohol or other drugs to temporarily make themselves feel better (Ellis, McInerney, DiGiuseppe and Yeager, 1988; Miller and Rollnick, 1991; Beck, Wright, Newman and Liese, 1993). Studies indicate that some people drink as a way of dealing with life's stressors (Alcohol and Stress, 1996). Drinking for these purposes is sometimes called "psychological dependency", though, as will be explained later, "dependency" has a somewhat different meaning in this model.

When someone obtains relief from dysphoria or some other type of discomfort, but does so in a way that does not alter the cause, they are said to be obtaining palliative relief. This is a negatively reinforced reward and people are inclined to repeat it in similar circumstances.

Again, the pharmacological effects will vary between people. The social environment and a person's personality will also influence a person's views as to whether or not drinking for palliative psychological relief is acceptable.

C. Escaping Withdrawal Effects

If a person drinks alcohol or uses certain other drugs in large quantities and over a long periods, their bodies change physically and adapt to the substance (Miller and

Rollnick, 1991). They get so that they need to use more of the substance in order to get the same good feelings that they used to get with far less (APA, 1994; Alcohol and Tolerance, 1995). This is called tolerance. Prolonged and heavy drinking will eventually cause most people to feel bad unless they keep some of the substance in their system (Alcohol Withdrawal Syndrome, 1989; APA, 1994; Cameron, 1995). This is the withdrawal phenomenon. Tolerance and withdrawal are often referred to as "physical dependency", though, again, "dependency" has a somewhat different meaning in this model.

Common symptoms include tremors, insomnia, vivid dreams, anxiety, agitation, irritability, loss of appetite, nausea, vomiting, headaches, sweating, seizers, hallucinations and the DT's (Saitz, 1998). Continued drinking, however, can temporarily relieve the withdrawal symptoms. Drinking to escape withdrawal makes continued use attractive. It becomes a habit that keeps withdrawal at bay, but at the cost of maintaining and deepening their withdrawal condition (APA, 1994; Cameron, 1995; Saitz, 1998).

The primary effect here is biological, but a person's social environment and personality contributes to how much pain and discomfort they are willing to tolerate. For example, a person is more likely to drink to avoid withdrawal pain if they believe that the withdrawal pain would be intolerable (Ellis, McInerney, DiGiuseppe and Yeager, 1988; Ellis and Velten, 1992; Beck, Wright, Newman and Liese, 1993).

D. Using Profiles

A person's using profile is derived from their affinity for using AOD in each of the three categories. For example, a person who is high in recreational/social use, low in psychological escape and without any use for withdrawal escape will behave entirely different and require different strategies for change from a person who is low in recreational/social use and high in both psychological and withdraw escape.

If a person with the former profile wants to change, they will just need to find other means to achieve their recreational and social needs. If a person with the latter profile wants to make changes, they will need to go through withdrawal. They will also need to practice (and possible develop) the cognitive and social skills necessary for successfully dealing with problems. They may also have to obtain psychotherapy and medication to deal with psychiatric disorders.

When it comes to the full range of PAOD, dichotomous thinking, such as assessing a person as an "alcoholic" or not, or assessing a person as a "drug addict" or not, is not helpful and is simplistic. Only a view that encompasses all of the factors that contribute to a person's place on the continuum will provide an accurate understanding of the nature of a person attraction to drinking, the degree of their attraction, their ambivalence and resistance to change, and what strategies will be necessary to reduce or eliminate their problems.

IV. PROBLEMS
A. Problematic/Self-Defeating Behavior

Any course of action results in an outcome or consequence. The intended outcomes are always to obtain something a person wants or to free them from something they do not want. Sometimes, the outcomes are as expected and sometimes they are not. Sometimes the outcomes are self-defeating or otherwise problematic.

The terms "self-defeating behaviors" and "problematic behaviors" are often used to mean the same thing, but there is at least one subtle difference. Any course of action that results in an outcome that prevents someone, the actor or others, from getting what they want is problematic behavior.

Self-defeating behavior, on the other hand, is a course of action that results in an outcome that does not get the actor what they want, regardless of how anyone else feels about the outcome. If an outcome is what the actor wanted, but the result is problematic to others, it is not self-defeating. If, however, the subsequent response from others has an outcome that the original actor does not like, it becomes self-defeating. Therefore, most problematic behaviors present a risk of becoming self-defeating.

As an example, if a husband loves to drink, but his wife does not want to be married to a drinker, drinking will be problematic (at least to the wife). Drinking is only self-defeating, in this example, if the husband does not want his wife to leave him. The term problematic will be used herein for both problematic and self-defeating.

Drinking is problematic, regardless of the situation or reward type, if it, directly or indirectly, interferes with obtaining one's aspirations (Ellis and Velten, 1992). Using illegal drugs always runs the risk of becoming self-defeating because of the possibilities of developing problems with the law.

B. Self-Perpetuating Problems

Problematic behaviors can become self-perpetuating, though that does not have to be the case. A self-perpetuating behavior is one in which the outcome is a cause of that behavior. An example related to palliative psychological relief might be, *I am sad because I drink too much and I drink too much because I'm sad.* Drinking to avoid withdrawal symptoms is also an example of a self-perpetuating problem.

C. Progressive Problems

Problematic behavior can also be progressive, though that does not have to be the case. Many of a person's aspirations are interrelated. A benefit to one aspiration can be a benefit to other aspirations. In the same way, interference with one aspiration may have negative repercussions in others. The degree to which a person's system of aspirations is interrelated determines the degree of progressiveness of a person's problems. Like in a chain reaction of dominos, problems in a highly integrated aspiration system can result in problems occurring more frequently, spreading into other areas of one's life or having consequences that are more serious.

For example, a person with progressive problems might say, *I drank a lot because I didn't like my job. The more I drank, the more my work performance suffered and the fewer choice assignments I received. That made me hate my job even more and I drank even more until I was fired. That was the last straw for my wife and she left me. After that, I drank even more until my liver was permanently damaged.*

D. Dependency

People can come to rely on drinking for a particular outcome, to the detriment of other means of achieving that outcome. Through neglect, abjuration and abandonment, a person may lose the knowledge, skills and resources to develop viable alternatives to drinking in many situations.

As defined herein, dependence means the loss of alternatives that have the same desired outcomes for that person as drinking does. Dependency is a matter of degree. The fewer perceived viable options a person feels they have, the greater their dependency on the substance. *I drink to have fun with my friends. Over the last few years, many of my friends, the ones who disapprove of the way I drink, no longer wanted to hang out with me. Only my drinking buddies are left and going to taverns seems like all I do for fun anymore.*

E. Intractability

PAOD can be defined as any AOD use that keeps a person from obtaining things that they value more than what alcohol and other drugs offers them. When PAOD is self-perpetuating, progressive or dependent, change becomes difficult. The more of these problem characteristics a person experiences the more intractable their problems become.

V. ADDICTION
A. Cravings

Imagine that an unethical scientist anesthetized a person without their knowledge or consent. While the subject was under, the evil scientist gave them alcohol until the subject became physically dependent. Since the subject was unconscious, they did not know what was happening to them. Then the scientist abruptly stopped the experiment. After the subject woke up, he started to experience withdrawal symptoms. Would the subject crave the drug to which he had become physically dependent?

Unless he had specific knowledge that related his bad feelings to withdrawal symptoms and specific knowledge that taking more of a particular substance would make him feel better, he would just think he was not feeling well and would not crave anything, there would be no appetitive urges to use any substance. However, if he had knowledge that a particular substance would release him from his bad feelings, he might desire or crave that substance.

Cravings, defined this way in regards to AOD, are the desires that arise from cognitive activities. The cognitive activities are constructed from specific knowledge of a substance's pleasure producing and relief providing powers, based on past experiences and beliefs. Thoughts about getting relief or obtaining pleasure through drinking generate the cravings (Relapse and Cravings, 1989).

There is no need for this experiment, it happens all the time when people leave the hospital after having been on certain pain medications (Beck, Wright, Newman and Liese, 1993). They often have withdrawal symptoms, but do not know that that is what they are experiencing. Since they do not know what is going on, they do not crave any drug.

Cravings have a narrow focus. They urge immediate gratification without consideration of the effects on other aspirations and long-term consequences.

B. Better Judgment

In contrast to cravings, a person's better judgment has an expansive focus. It arises from the knowledge and thoughts concerned with maximizing everything that is important to a person, now and over time, not just with what they are occupied with at the moment.

C. Addiction

If the perceived costs of drinking exceed the perceived rewards, a person's better judgment will tell them to quit or cut back. Most people do just that, with or without treatment (Miller and Rollnick, 1991; National Institute of Health, 1998). Other people however, repeatedly try to cut back or quit and repeatedly fail. Their better judgment tells them that they need to make changes, but when it comes time to act, their cravings win out. They struggle between their craving-generating thoughts and their better judgment-driven thoughts, choosing immediate gratification at the expense of other valued-things.

There is an element of difference that separates those who act on their better judgment and those who yield to their cravings without consideration to other things of value and long-term consequences. That element is the mental state of addiction.

Addiction, as defined herein, is a mental state in which a person realizes that alcohol or other drugs are causing them more problems than what they are worth and want to quit or cut back, but keeps changing their mind and keeps on using. They struggle between thoughts and feelings that urge them to use and others that say not to. In the mean time, their problems get worse and worse. Addiction is what people often think of when they say someone is "hooked."

Addiction is not synonymous with drinking to escape withdrawal effects, though that is frequently a factor when addiction is present. A person may not consider their withdrawal discomforts self-defeating and have no desire to cut back or quit. To them, drinking to escape withdrawal effects is just the price they have to pay to do what they want to do. These people are not addicted, they are just using to escape withdrawal effects.

The same holds true for recreational/social users and for using for palliative psychological relief. They may or may not be addicted. They may or may not want to make changes.

VI. DECISION-MAKING
A. Automatic/ deliberate Information Processing and Decision-Making

> In a very real sense we have two minds, one that thinks and
> one that feels.
>
> *Emotional Intelligence*
> Daniel Goleman

> Right now, you are feeling your addiction. And you are
> having conflicting thoughts about the use of alcohol. You

are *ambivalent* about drinking, something *all* addicted people have in common. On the one hand, you would like to stop drinking and get on with your life, but on the other hand, you are terrified of giving up alcohol. That part of you wants to drink forever.

Rational Recovery:
The New Cure for Substance Addiction
Jack Trimpey

Many of the factors that contribute to PAOD result from a person's high degree of attraction to their substance. The stronger their attraction, the greater their ambivalence and the more difficult it is for them act in ways consistent with their better judgment. However, just because something is difficult does not explain why a person would persistently do something in which the costs exceed the rewards. Why do PAOD users not cut back or quit in the face of persistent problems? The answer is to be found, in part, in the automatic/deliberate nature of how humans process information and make decisions.

One of Steve Martin's funnier movies is *All of Me* in which he starred with Lily Tomlin. In the movie, Tomlin plays a rich woman who has been sick most of her life. She is on the verge of death and has hired a swami to transmigrate her soul into the body of a healthy young woman, whose soul would then be released into the universal bliss. Unfortunately, Tomlin's soul accidentally ends up inside Steve Martin's body, with Martin still in it. The sight gags that follow are hilarious, as the two separate minds try to get Martin's body to do different things at the same time.

Of course, things like this do not happen in real life. A person has only one mind to direct one action at a time. However, it sometimes seems as if we have two people inside of us, one that feels strongly about doing one thing and another that thinks that doing something else might be a better idea.

Perhaps you experienced a struggle of this nature the last time you were thinking about buying a new car. Part of you wanted the little red sports car. Sports cars are fast, sexy and really really neat. You just had to have it. However, another part of you wanted to slow down and think things through before you decided what to buy. *How much would it cost? What kind of gas mileage would it get? How much would insurance be? Would it be hard to get repairs?* And so on.

Human decision-making can be understood using the metaphor that people have two minds. The automatic mind processes information and makes decisions automatically and is experienced through emotions. The deliberate mind uses non-automatic information processing and decision-making and is experienced through conscious verbal thought.[1] For the most part, the two minds work together harmoniously to decide how we should respond to life's events, but not always. Many personal problems, especially those that are a consequence of problematic alcohol and other drug use, can be understood as a conflict between the two minds and a person's inability to resolve this conflict in favor of their better judgment.

B. Automatic Mind

> All organisms with complex nervous systems are faced
> with the moment-by-moment question that is posed by life:
> What shall I do next?

---

[1] To paraphrase Steven Pinker (1997), the mind is just one of the things that the brain does. The academic debate over what the mind actually is will be difficult to settle. Each discipline and the people within those disciplines mean something different when they use the term. What is being said here is that the brain processes information in stages – sequentially and in parallel. It makes decisions and urges behaviors at various stages of processing. Sometimes these decisions are compatable. Sometimes they are not. Much of the information processing can be grouped as belonging to automatic processing subsystems and the rest can be grouped as belonging to deliberate processing subsystems. A person 's behavior can be described in terms of which subsystem most influences behavior in a particular situation. Understanding the differences between the subsystems and how they function, allows people to exercise some control over them and the outcomes of their behavior. Using the terms automatic mind and deliberate mind is just a literary conveniences. This should not be a problem as long as we keep in mind that they are metaphors used to describe portions of a complex system of information processing and decision-making.

Kanzi: The Ape at the Brink of the Human Mind
Sue Savage-Rumbaugh and Roger Lewin

Metaphorically speaking, both the automatic mind and the deliberate mind are constantly scanning the environment to decide what we should do next. They look for opportunities to obtain what we want and to keep us free from things that we do not want. However, they each do this in significantly different ways.

The automatic mind evolved a long time ago, when our ancestors lived in a world where decisions needed to be made quickly (Ekman, 1992; Epstein and Brodsky, 1993; Epstein, 1994, 1998; LeDoux, 1996, 2002). If our ancestors did not act fast, their dinner would escape. If they were too slow, they would become dinner for some fierce beast. If humans, then and now, had to stop and reason everything out before they acted, they would get little else done and would not be very successful with life's many challenges (LeDoux, 1996). The simple thoughts of AOD pleasures and relief come to mind swiftly, while complex thoughts about consequences and responsibilities take time to form.

A person's automatic mind has a very limited view of the world (Epstein and Brodsky, 1993). It is close-minded. It stubbornly resists information that contradicts the way it feels. It is shortsighted and single-minded. It only offers solutions for the immediate situation, the surface problem. The automatic mind does not consider the long-term consequences or how the behaviors its emotions are urging might affect a person's overall aspirations (Tice, Bratslavsky and Baumeister, 2001). The desire to use in spite of persistent negative consequences is an expression of the shortsightedness and single-mindedness of the automatic mind.

If the automatic mind has determined that something undesirable is about to happen, such as when something threatens an aspiration, the brain normally prepares itself and the body to fight the threat or run away from it. This is the so-called "fight or flight response" (Epstein and Brodsky, 1993; Epstein, 1998). If the automatic mind decides to put a stop to the menace, it prepares to confront it with intimidation or force. When conscious attention is focused on these preparations, a person experiences anger or related emotions (LeDoux, 1996; McGuire and Troisi, 1998; Epstein, 1998).

If, on the other hand, the automatic mind concludes that it probably cannot stop the threat, it prepares for and urges escape. When conscious attention is focused on these preparations, a person experiences fear or related emotions (LeDoux, 1996; Epstein, 1998; McGuire and Troisi, 1998).

If the automatic mind does not know what to do in a threatening situation, it freezes the body and attention is focused on the situation. A person remains in this state until the threat goes away, until the situation forces action or until some other opportunity to end the threat appears. When conscious attention is focused on this state, a person experiences anxiety or related emotions (LeDoux, 1996, 2002; McGuire and Troisi, 1998).

There are also times when struggling makes a threatening situation worse. If the automatic mind has reached this conclusion, a person will surrender. They try to disengage from their environment to minimize damage and give themselves time to heal (Epstein and Brodsky, 1993). Surrender is experienced as sadness or related emotions (Epstein and Brodsky, 1993; LeDoux, 1996; McGuire and Troisi, 1998).

If the automatic mind, on the other hand, obtains a thing of value or senses an opportunity to do so, a person will experience a feeling of either power/control/elation or of pleasure/satisfaction/joy (McGuire and Troisi, 1998). Power/control/elation are associated with mastery and the emotional urges to dominate a situation in order to obtain something of value. In contrast, pleasure/satisfaction/joy, among other things, are associated with a sense of well-being, security and freedom from harm and the emotional urges that enhance social cooperation.

McGuire and Troisi make an interesting observation concerning positive emotions and drug use (1998). Stimulants like cocaine and amphetamine are dopamine-influencing drugs and are often associated with competitive and agonistic social interactions. They appear to be related to the feelings of power/control/elation. On the other hand, drugs that influence the opiod-reward system, such as heroin, appear to increase affiliative behaviors and likely related to the feelings of pleasure/satisfaction/joy.

The automatic mind is built up from instinctual-like feelings, past experiences and beliefs in the form of habitual thoughts (Lazarus and Folkman, 1984; Ekman, 1992; Epstein and Brodsky, 1993; Damasio 1994; Epstein, 1994, 1998; McGuire and Troisi, 1998). Furthermore, the actions urged by the automatic mind may be helpful or unhelpful in dealing with life's problems (Epstein, 1994; McGuire and Troisi, 1998). They can be realistic and useful or unrealistic and self-defeating.

With instinctual-like feelings, people are biologically predisposed to respond to some things and to certain situations in a stereotypical way, because that is the way their brains are wired (Ekman, 1992; Epstein and Brodsky, 1993; Epstein, 1994, 1998; McGuire and Troisi, 1998; LeDoux, 2002). LeDoux provides an example offered by Darwin's own experience that illustrates instinctual-like responses (1996, p. 112):

> I put my face close to the thick glass-plate in front of a puff-adder in the Zoological Gardens, with the firm determination of not starting back if the snake struck at me; but, as soon as the blow was struck, my resolution went for nothing, and I jumped a yard or two backwards with astonishing rapidity. My will and reason were powerless against the imagination of a danger which had never been experienced.

The automatic mind is also driven by past experiences. Once a person has had an emotionally significant experience, they tend to feel the same way later in similar situations and are emotionally urged to respond as they did then (Epstein and Brodsky, 1993; Epstein, 1994, 1998; LeDoux, 2002). We learn through experience what things cause pain and pleasure and use those experiences as guides for future behavior.

The automatic mind also operates with habitual beliefs (Ellis and Harper, 1961; Burns, 1980; Epstein and Brodsky, 1993; Epstein 1994, 1998; Beck, 1995). People form generalized ideas that explain how things work, how they "should" personally act in certain situations and how other people "should" behave in certain situations (Ellis and Harper, 1961; Lazarus and Folkman, 1984; Epstein and Brodsky, 1993; Epstein, 1994, 1998; Bandura, Barbaranelli, Caprara and Pastorelli, 1996; McGuire and Troisi, 1998). If those thoughts are repeated frequently, they become automatic or habitual beliefs and a person is urged to act as they direct without having to consciously think them first.

The automatic mind makes decisions and solves problems by automatically deciding what is going on and automatically deciding what to do about it (Ekman, 1992; Epstein and Brodsky, 1993; LeDoux, 1996). There is no thinking. There are no choices, things just flow.

If our ancestors ran away from a threatening beast, they solved their problem and their automatic mind served them well. If a man runs away from a problem with his spouse, either literally by leaving or figuratively by ignoring it or by drinking, his problems are still there waiting for him. If our ancestors killed the beast, they solved their problem and their automatic mind served them well. If a man hits his spouse, he increases his problems. The behaviors urged by strong emotions are easily problematic in our modern complex world (Arnsten, 1998; Epstein, 1998).

C. Deliberate mind

The deliberate mind evolved later than the automatic mind (Epstein, 1998; McGuire and Troisi, 1998). It is integrated with and works in parallel with the automatic mind. For the most part, they work together in harmony. However, there are times when they are at odds, which can decrease a person's level of competency (Goleman, 1995; Epstein, 1998).

The deliberate mind is slower than the automatic mind. It has more neurological activity to perform before it makes a decision (Goleman, 1995, Epstein and Brodsky, 1993). Often the automatic mind has already urged a response before the deliberate mind has even begun to register what is going on. Often the automatic mind urgings for the deep pleasures of drinking have already begun to take hold before the deliberate mind has even begun to consider the consequences.

Furthermore, the deliberate mind is less compelling and less intense than the automatic mind. Reason does not carry the blind confidence that emotions do (LeDoux, 1996). *I know a drink will make me feel better. I might have a problem if I do though.*

The deliberate mind can be patient, whereas the automatic mind is not. It does not urge action until it has figured out what it believes is the best course of action. It is open-minded and is not resistive to further information.

Unlike the automatic mind that is shortsighted and single minded, the deliberate mind is concerned with long-term as well as short-term goals (Epstein and Brodsky,

1993). It is concerned with not only the particular aspiration that is at stake in any situation, but also with a person's overall aspirations.

The deliberate mind can put up with discomfort in the short-term if it sees a greater good to be received later. The automatic mind does not respond this way easily, if at all, and more often seeks immediate gratification (Tice, Bratslavsky and Baumeister, 2001). The automatic mind creates discomfort when it is deprived of something it wants. *I can't stand this. I've gotta have a drink right now. I don't care what anyone thinks.* The deliberate mind can better tolerate discomfort. *I can't drink on duty. I'll just wait until after work.*

The deliberate mind is known to us primarily through our conscious verbal thoughts (LeDoux, 1996; Epstein, 1998). It can make decisions by exploring what is really going on, rather than just reacting to perceptions like the automatic mind does (LeDoux, 2002). The deliberate mind can generate options for different ways to respond to a problem, rather than just reacting to it in a predetermined way (Damasio, 1994; McGuire and Troisi, 1998; LeDoux, 2002). The deliberate mind can weigh out the options it has generated to determine which will most likely produce the best results under the circumstances. When functioning most effectively, it seeks the choice that will solve the problem in a way that has the fewest costs and the most rewards with respect to all of the things of which a person is concerned (Damasio, 1994). It is the process by which one's better judgment may be formulated.[2]

VII. DYSREASONING EFFECTS
A. Dominance of deliberate mind

---

[2] Lack of complete knowledge and degree of intelligence also affect the outcome, but as long as that is acknowledged, it need not be discussed in detail.

> Man is not disturbed by events, but by the view he takes of
> them.
>
> Epictetus

Even though the automatic mind is faster, more intense and more confident of itself than the deliberate mind, the deliberate mind has the potential, in most cases, to determine a person's behavior (LeDoux, 2002). This is because emotional urges only last for a few seconds, unless the continued presence of the stimulus keeps reactivating them (Ekman 1992; McGuire and Troisi, 1998). Once the stimulus disappears, the emotion fades quickly. It is usually a person's thoughts that keep an emotion active long after the original stimulus is gone.

To give an example of this, imagine that you are in heavy traffic. A car cuts in front of you and then heads off an exit ramp. You might have an initial instinct-like reaction of fear, but it fades in seconds. However, you might start thinking: *That goddamn son-of-a-bitch! Who does he think he is? I'd like to teach that little asshole a thing or two!* If so, you will generate angry feelings and emotional urges to punish the perpetrator. If you keep those thoughts up you will put yourself into a bad mood, striking out at other people with little or no cause.

On the other hand, you might stop your angry thoughts and replace them with something like: *Just because he's an irresponsible driver, I don't have to act like a jerk too. I'm not going to let this spoil my day.* If you do this, you will calm down and your mood and thoughts will return to normal.

It was the same event that created the two different sets of feelings and urges, a car cutting in front of you. What made a difference in how you felt and what you did was how you explained the event to yourself (Ellis and Harper, 1961; Burns, 1980; Freeman and DeWolf, 1992; Epstein and Brodsky, 1993; Epstein, 1994, 1998; Beck, 1995). If your thoughts dwelled on the perpetrator, you became angry and might have struck out at him or anyone else who later interfered with your activities. If your thoughts did not dwell on the incident, if you instead decided that there was nothing to gain and maybe something to lose by becoming aroused over something you could not change, you would have calmed down and continued on with the business at hand.

For the most part, people who manage their thoughts are in control of how they feel and how they act. They use their deliberate mind to figure out the most likely explanation for events and then choose a course of action that is most useful in relation to their overall aspirations – in both the short and long-term.

There are circumstances, however, in which the ability of the deliberate mind to determine behavior can be diminished or eliminated altogether (Epstein and Brodsky, 1993). These processes are herein called the dysreasoning effects and are a major cause of poor decision-making, especially for PAOD use (Miller and Rollnick, 1991).

B. Impulsivity

Some people are prone to impulsivity; their automatic mind jumps them into action before their deliberate mind even have a chance to get started. David Keirsey has categorized this temperament as sensory perceivers and refers to them as Artisans (1998). People of this temperament are not only impulsive, but trust their impulses and feel frustrated if they are restrained from acting on them, even if doing so has been a source of problems for them in the past.

In addition, people under stress tend to be impulsive, regardless of their temperament (LeDoux, 1996, 2002; Arnstein, 1998; Tice, Bratslavsky and Baumeister, 2001).

When you are stressed, you cannot think clearly and are driven more by how you feel than by reason. The dysreasoning effect caused by stress probably corresponds to the "hunger" and "tired" elements of Alcoholic Anonymous' HALT (hunger, anger, loneliness and tired) relapse warning.

C. Emotional Hijacking

Another dysreasoning effect is an emotional hijacking (Epstein and Brodsky, 1993; LeDoux, 1996, 2002; Arnstein, 1998). Some situations get people so emotionally overwhelmed that they cannot think straight and their emotions carry them away. When their automatic mind declares an emergency, their deliberate mind's ability to function is compromised. Acting in a rage is an example. After a person calms down and reason returns, they wonder what came over them.

D. Clouded Judgment

Clouded judgment and moods are another significant dysreasoning effect (Epstein and Brodsky, 1993; Epstein, 1994, 1998; LeDoux, 2002). Rather than seeking confirming evidence for their interpretation of events, they just feel confident that they know what is going on. Rather than formulating a variety of choices, they only create options consistent with their current state of emotions. Their moods bias their decision-making. For example, when a person is sad, they feel powerless and lose confidence in their abilities. They do not attempt activities that they might normally pursue. The dysreasoning effect caused by clouded judgment probably corresponds to the "anger" and "loneliness" elements of the HALT relapse warning.

E. Self-Defeating Beliefs

Another dysreasoning effect is self-defeating beliefs (Ellis and Harper, 1961; Epstein and Brodsky, 1993; Epstein, 1994, 1998; Beck, 1995). Beliefs of this type limit a person's thinking by providing irrational, inflexible responses to life's situations, instead of developing effective solutions in an ever-changing environment. Rather than being resilient and creative, they do things a certain way every time, whether that way is useful or not.

The cognitive therapist Albert Ellis and his Rational-Emotive Behavioral Therapy holds that irrational self-talk causes people to suffer needlessly and to be unnecessarily ineffective (1961). The heart of irrational self-talk is the habitual assumptions that some events are too "awful" to deal with or that a person "absolutely" has to respond to certain situations in a specific way (Davis, Eshelman and McKay, 1988).

REBT sees "low frustration tolerance" as the primary factor causing and maintaining addiction (Ellis, McInerney, DiGiuseppe and Yeager, 1988). Irrational beliefs such as *I cannot stand it when I cannot drink* or *I'm not strong enough to resist alcohol* cause a sense of frustration and a deemed inability to manage one's self.

The psychiatrist Aaron Beck developed a systematic description of the origins of irrational beliefs called Cognitive Therapy (1995). It puts forth the idea that every event is followed by an automatic thought. The automatic thought leads to an emotional and behavioral reaction. The thought has its origin in intermediate beliefs that consist of rules, attitudes and assumptions. The intermediate beliefs, in turn, are expressions of core beliefs.

For example, a man is given an assignment at work – the event. His automatic thoughts might be, *This is hard. I'll never be able to do it. Then they'll really think I'm stupid.* These automatic thoughts make him feel sad and he puts off starting the assignment and goes drinking instead – emotional and behavioral responses. His intermediate belief might be something like, *If something is difficult, it means I'm stupid.* And, *If I feel bad, I need a few drinks to feel better.* The core belief that gives rise to it all might be, "I'm incompetent."

Judith Beck, in her book *Cognitive Therapy: Basic and Beyond* (1995), lists five basic self-defeating core beliefs. Two of them predispose people to feel bad about themselves: "I'm incompetent" and "I'm unlovable." The other three predispose them to have problems with others: "The world is a rotten place," "You can't trust anyone" and "Everyone is out to hurt me."

Cognitive Therapy holds that "the web of external and internal problems leading to and later maintaining compulsive drug use is the defining characteristic of addiction" (Beck, Wright, Newman and Liese, 1993, p. 23). Treatment involves uncovering the dysfunctional beliefs that cause a person's problems and lead them to believe that drinking is the solution to their problems. Once they are found to be irrational, they will lose their control over a person's behavior and allow the creation of a stronger system of internal controls.

Rational Recovery offers a list of commonly held beliefs, while not necessarily irrational, mislead a user into feeling that their options are limited (Trimpey, 1996). For example, a person may believe that they need to use in order to relax. They think, *After a hard day, I want to have a drink and feel good.* Trimpey points out in this example that instead of using natural skills to relax and enjoy one's self, they choose the pleasures of using and then believe that they cannot relax without their drug (1996). See table 1 for a full list of these beliefs.

Albert Bandura and colleagues add to this with their Moral Disengagement theory (1996). Their research supports the idea that people develop a set of rules concerning what is "right and wrong" and obey them in order to avoid the bad feelings that they would have about themselves if they violated them. However, people sometimes justify behaviors that harm others or themselves by making exceptions to those rules. These exceptions neutralize the self-censorship and allow them to act contrary to their rules of morality and still feel good about themselves.

There are several neutralizing strategies. One example is "advantageous comparison" in which a person compares their activities with others that are flagrantly more reprehensible (Bandura, Barbaranelli, Caprara and Pastorelli, 1996). The contrast makes their behavior seem mild in comparison. *I only drove after a few beers. It's not like I robbed a bank or something.* See table 2 for a complete list of neutralizing strategies.

This is particularly instructive in that AOD users must sometimes choose between drinking and doing something else of value. If they choose drinking and the other aspiration is harmed, the use of neutralizing thoughts allows them to not feel bad about it. This makes drinking become more entrenched at the expense of other aspirations. The discussion of the erosions of aspirations resulting from the use of neutralizing strategies will cover this in more detail.

F. Avoidance Strategies

Another dysreasoning effect is related to avoidance strategies. As discussed earlier, the emotions people often experience when things are not going their way are anger, sadness, fear and anxiety. These emotions can be the results of their automatic thoughts and in turn, lead to the development of habitual avoidance strategies that result in a person neglecting the sources of their problems (LeDoux, 1996)

A person's thoughts might be: *This is awful and there is nothing I can do about it.* Those thoughts might make a person feel sad and see themselves as powerless. As a result, they will just give up and do nothing to solve their problems. *What's the use of trying to stay sober, I can't help myself.*

A person might think: *This is bad and I don't know what to do.* This will make them feel anxious and ruminate, rather than act. Drinking then becomes attractive as a relief from this stress (Tiffany, 1999).

A person might think: T*his is awful - I've just got to get away.* These thoughts will make them experience fear and feel like running away, literally or in their heads. They can easily rationalize, minimize, intellectualize and procrastinate rather than trying to solve their problems. *Sure, I drink some, but it's not really that bad.*

They might have thoughts like, *This is not fair - he'll pay for doing that.* Some people feel angry and see others as the source of their problems. They will believe that others need to change, not themselves, before a situation can get better. As a result, they will not take constructive actions to solve their problems (Lazarus and Folkman, 1984; Bandura, Barbaranelli, Caprara and Pastorelli, 1996). Other angry people may become aggressive and risk retribution from others. *To hell with them, I don't care what they think. I'll drink if I want to.*

Another avoidance strategy is to seek palliative relief (Epstein and Brodsky, 1993; Tice, Bratslavsky and Baumeister, 2001). People sometimes do things that make them feel good, at least temporarily, but that do not address the source of the problem (Goleman, 1995; Bandura, Barbaranelli, Caprara and Pastorelli, 1996). They overeat, gamble, shop, or use alcohol and other drugs. They may do something that makes them feel dominant and powerful. They kick the dog or yell at the kids.

G. Alcohol and Other Drugs

Alcohol and other intoxicating drugs can also lead to a dysreasoning effect by altering brain functions (Alcohol and Cognition, 1989; Epstein and Brodsky, 1993; Alcohol-Related Impairment, 1994; APA, 1994). While alcohol and other intoxicating drugs affect all brain functioning, they tend to diminish higher cognitive functions quicker and to a greater extent than they do lower brain functions (Fishman, 1986). This leaves only the automatic mind to make decisions and if it wants to drink, there is no deliberate mind to control it.

H. Mental Disorders

Mental disorders can also be a dysreasoning effect. For example, schizophrenia and bipolar disorder can compromise a person's information processing and other functional capacities (McGuire and Troisi, 1998). A person with an active disorder may not have ability to make rational decisions and in that sense their decisions can be viewed an irresistible compulsions.

E. Emotionally Biased Thoughts

In any particular situation, a person may encounter internal or external cues related to past rewarding recreational and social experiences, to past psychologically distressing situations or to withdrawal effects. These cues can trigger, in the automatic mind, feelings and vague urges to act upon them. These feelings, however, last for only a few seconds, unless they are re-triggered by their internal or external cues (Ekman, 1992; McGuire and Troisi, 1998). In the absence of the cues, the feelings just fade away.

Shortly after these feelings are triggered, a person with specific knowledge of AOD's pleasure producing and relief providing powers might experience, in their deliberate mind, conscious verbal thoughts, however fleeting, that produce cravings to drink or use. If that person also has knowledge that AOD has caused them more harm than rewards, they will experience conscious verbal thoughts that urge restraint and dampen the cravings, unless they are under the influence of dysreasoning effects. If they are under the influence of dysreasoning effects, these dampening thoughts will be superseded by emotionally biased thoughts that support the cravings.

With no mental process to mitigate them, the undampened cravings will drive them to seek the short-term gratification of drinking or using without consideration of the long-term effects on their overall aspirations. The person will drink or use unless some external force prevents it from happening or unless the dysreasoning effects are attenuated.

VIII. ASPIRATIONS AND EFFICACY
A. Efficacy

Figure 2 graphically represents our ability to obtain our overall aspirations. This ability is called "efficacy." If a person is doing a good job at getting what they want, or expects to do well, they would be near the top of the line. If a person is doing a poor job, or believe that they will do poorly, they would be lower down the line. This is a measure of their situational competency.

46

FIGURE 2.

EFFICACY

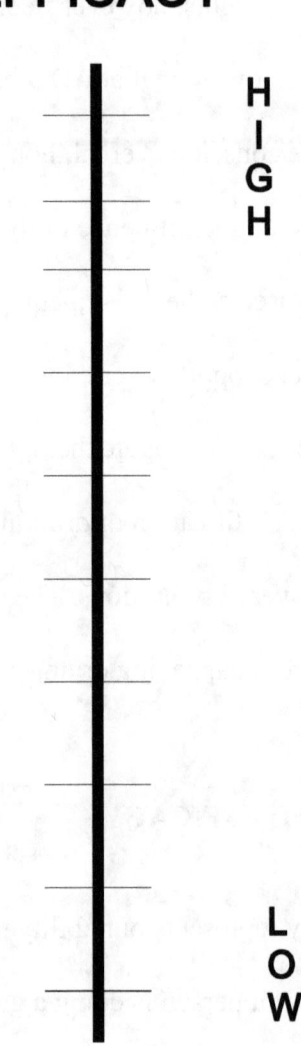

B. Relationship Between Aspirations and Efficacy

Putting the aspiration scale and efficacy scale together creates a graphic representation of the dynamic relationship between a person's aspirations and their sense of efficacy. See figure 3.

If a person's overall aspirations are high and they are doing well in obtaining them, they experience power/control/elation, pleasure/satisfaction/joy or a general sense of well-being, happiness or fulfillment. The primary reasons for high efficacy are well-adjusted aspirations and the lack of dysreasoning effects. This is indicative of living in accordance with one's better judgment. See Figure 3.

Having high aspirations, but lowered efficacy makes a person feel sad, anger, fearful, anxious or a general sense of being unhappy or unfulfilled. A primary reason for lowered efficacy are holding on to aspirations that are either not realistically obtainable or that are not harmoniously integrated. Dysreasoning effects are another reason for lowered efficacy. See Figure 3. This is indicative of a person who is "out of control." They are living with their automatic mind in charge while their deliberate mind is reduced in effectiveness by dysreasoning effects.

IX. REDUCED EFFICACY
A. Problem Solving

> Predictions are difficult, especially about the future
> Yogi Berra

> God grant me the Serenity to
> accept the things I cannot change
> Courage to change the things I can
> and the Wisdom to know the difference.
> Serenity Prayer

FIGURE 3.

ASPIRATIONS   EFFICACY

Combined Aspirations Scale &

Efficacy Scale

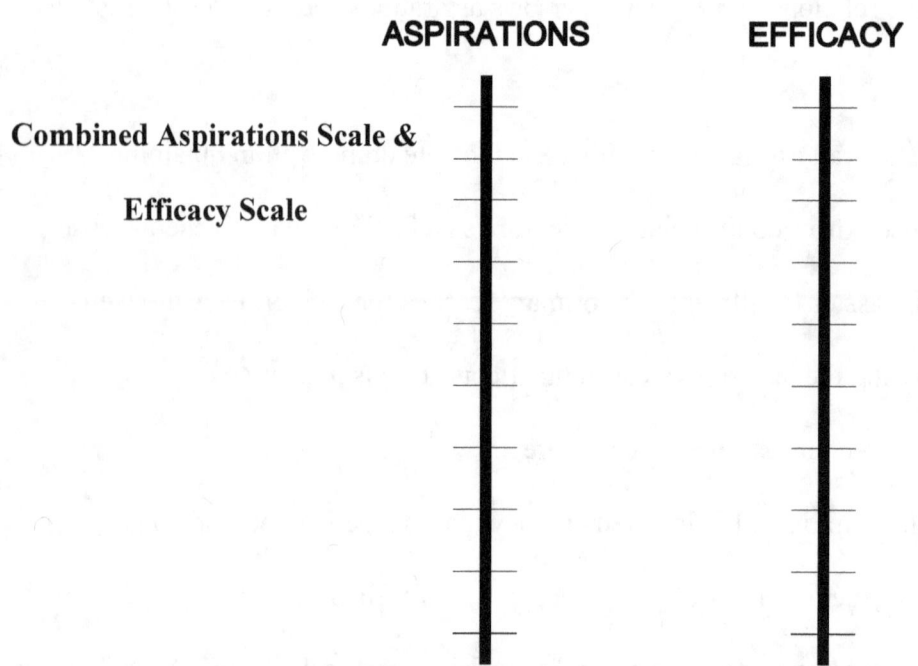

High Aspirations & High Efficacy   High Aspirations & Lowered Efficacy

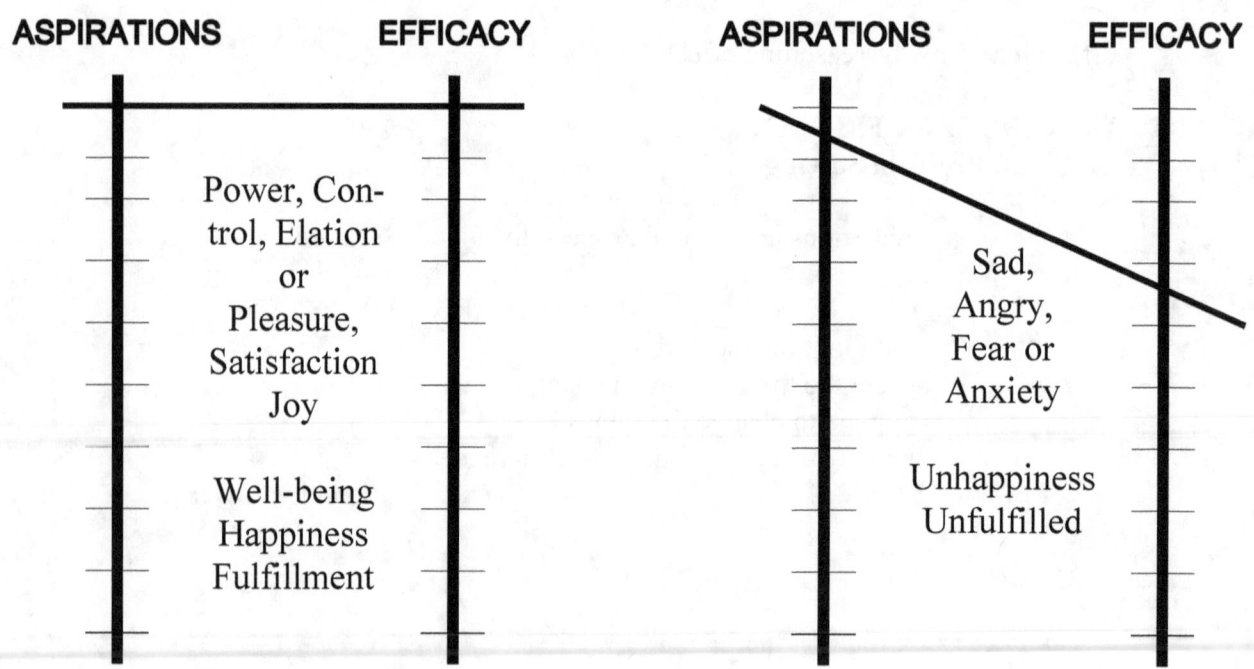

ASPIRATIONS   EFFICACY

Power, Control, Elation or Pleasure, Satisfaction Joy

Well-being Happiness Fulfillment

ASPIRATIONS   EFFICACY

Sad, Angry, Fear or Anxiety

Unhappiness Unfulfilled

When a person is not getting what they want, they have three choices: problem solving, coping or muddling-through (Lazarus and Folkman, 1984; McGuire and Troisi, 1998). Problem solving means fixing the problem so that a person gets what they want, either now or in the future (Damasio, 1994). Problem solving means changing things in the world outside us and restoring efficacy. For example, *If I can't drink like a gentleman, I won't drink at all*. Changing the things that we can change, as the Serenity Prayer petitions, is problem solving.

B. Coping

There are times, however, when a person is not getting what they want and problem solving is not a useful strategy because every solution has a poor cost/reward ratio or the goal unachievable. For example, you might want to go drinking with the boys Saturday night, but you promised your wife that you would go to the symphony. You cannot have it both ways, so you have to choose.

To some people, coping means any adaptive response to a situation, be it problem solving or an emotional reappraisal (Lazarus and Folkman, 1984; Begley, 1998). As used herein, coping means to change the inside world so that one's bad feelings are diminished (Lazarus and Folkman, 1984; Epstein and Brodsky, 1993; Begley, 1998,). Coping means reappraising one's aspirations. It means wanting something less or giving up on something that cannot be obtained (Festinger, 1957). Coping means taking a realistic view of your aspirations and in so doing allowing them to readjust themselves into a realistic balance, restoring your efficacy. It means getting one's priorities straight. Accepting the things we cannot change, as the Serenity prayer partitions, is coping.

C. Erosion of Aspirations

There are aspects of coping that can result in the erosion of one's aspirations, however (McCarthy and Stewart, 1998). Classical cognitive dissonance theory suggests that making a decision between mutually exclusive, nearly equal valued-things creates cognitive dissonance and that people tend to act in ways that reduce its discomfort (Festinger, 1957).

For example, a man may have to choose between a night of drinking and a night of playing cards with a non-drinking friend. He would like to do both, but cannot and must choose. If he chooses drinking, he would feel bad about disappointing his friend. He could reduce this dissonance by telling himself that he will play cards with his friend the next time. If he keeps his promise, he would be exercising the mutually reciprocal trade-off style of a well-adjusted system of aspiration and his aspirations would remain stable and harmonious. However, if he continues to drink at the expense of his friend, he would eventually change his beliefs in regards to drinking and his friend to eliminate the disso-nance. He would increase the value of drinking with thoughts like, *Drinking is more fun than playing cards.* He would devalue his association with his friend with thoughts like, *Non-drinkers are such a drag.* See figure 4.

The theory goes on to say that these new beliefs would be reinforced by seeking out and associating with like-minded people, as well as by seeking out information that supports the new beliefs, while discounting contradictory information.

Drinking would take on a new, higher priority over some of a person's other aspi-rations that were previously of greater value. Without mutually reciprocating trade-offs, the process can snowball, creating instability within one's system of aspirations and

FIGURE 4.

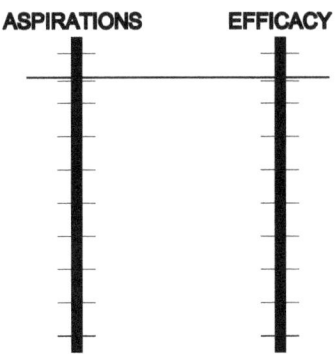

Everything is going OK.

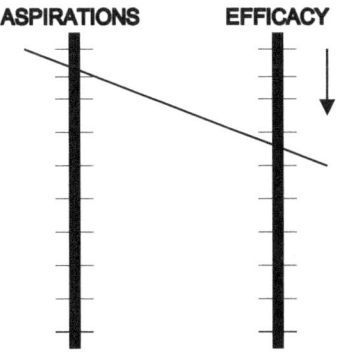

Fight with wife over drinking. Everything is not OK now. Efficacy drops.

Cognitive dissonance. (Values wife less now) Less fulfilled and more unhappy.

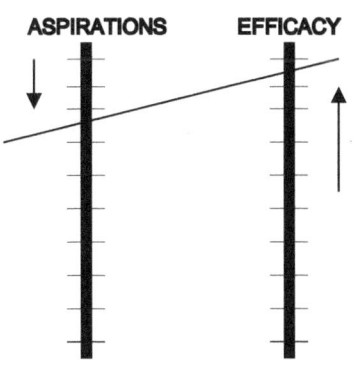

Blames wife for the fight. Uses neutralizing thoughts "Stupid woman." Efficacy returns.

Cognitive dissonance neutralized. (Values drinking more – at expense of valuing wife less). More likely to drink in the future with less concern over wife's feelings.

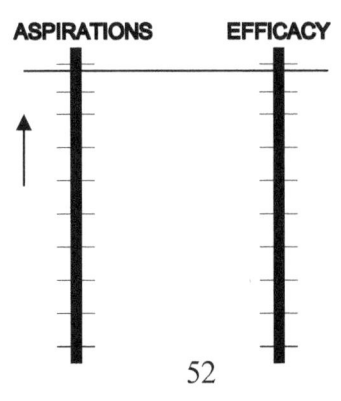

New beliefs that reinforce drinking. "I have a right to let off a little steam once in a while." Everything is OK again.

ever-increasing AOD use while other aspirations erode in value. It can become self-per-petuating, progressive and create dependencies.

This can be even more dramatic if poor cost/reward decisions are made under the dysreasoning effect of AOD use. For example, a man may value his family's well-being many times over his drinking pleasures. However, if he blows his paycheck on alcohol while under the influence, he will experience great dissonance. This can be ameliorated by promising never to do such a stupid thing again. If he fails to keep his promise, he will eventually neutralize the bad feelings with a set of new beliefs that justify and give license to his behavior (Ellis and Velten, 1992; Bandura, Barbaranelli, Caprara and Pastorelli, 1996). *I am not such a bad father. I don't hit my kids. People expect too much from me. I have a right to blow off a little steam.* These are neutralizing thoughts and avoidance strategies based on anger.

Or, he can follow a different route and lose confidence in his ability to control his behavior. He sees himself as a bad person and feels hopeless and powerless over his behavior (Ellis, McInerney, DiGiuseppe and Yeager, 1988). His new beliefs support the idea that he cannot help him himself when it comes to drinking and he might as well not even try. These are neutralizing thoughts and avoidance strategies based on sadness.

In either case, there would be an accelerated increase in drinking, as well as a dramatic decline in the value of his other aspirations.

D. Muddling-Through

It is difficult to predict the future and what changes will or will not lead to desired outcomes. It is difficult to know when to problem solve and when to cope. This is true in all aspects of life, not just with PAOD. However, many people under these circumstances are not really looking for solutions, they are muddling-through.

Muddling-through is the third strategy for dealing with problems and is driven by seeking palliative relief and other avoidance strategies. It is used by some people when they do not like a situation, but takes no action to fix it or learns to live with it (Epstein and Brodsky, 1993). Some problems occur once and then do not return. Under these circumstances, muddling-through might not be a bad choice. However, many problems reoccur if they are not dealt with effectively and can become chronic (Freeman and De-Wolf, 1992).

X. REDUCING PROBLEMATIC ALCOHOL AND OTHER DRUG USE
A. Confrontation

> The only way to get rid of a temptation is to yield to it. Resist it, and your soul grows sick with longing for the things it has forbidden itself.
> *The Picture of Dorian Gray*
> Oscar Wilde

What is a person to do when their alcohol or other drug use becomes a problem for them or for those around them? How is it to be dealt with?

Traditional approaches have consisted of breaking down an "alcoholic's" denial with confrontation (Miller and Rollnick, 1991). Once the person has made a decision for abstinence, they are set on a lifelong journey of working their program.

Some people see the light when confronted and accept the need for change. This is unlikely, though, unless there already is an established caring relationship between the parties. Most people become defensive when confronted (Miller and Rollnick, 1991). Many PAOD users in treatment agree on the outside, but disagree on the inside. They say what they need to say in order to get through their treatment ordeal, but do not make intrinsic changes. Others resist when confronted and a power struggles ensues. In either case, the patient usually ends up defending the very opposite ideas from what that the treatment provider is trying to make them consider. This entrenches problematic beliefs and makes change even less likely.

B. Stages of Change

Some people's drinking is problematic to others, but is not considered problematic by the users. As long as they rationally and deliberately consider all of the negative consequences as being an acceptable price for them to pay in order for them to do what they want to do, there are no problems for them that require change. Their AOD is not a treatment issue. If their behavior is illegal, it is a criminal issue. If it is not illegal, it is a civil liberty issue.

On the other hand, there are some people whose drinking is problematic to others and to themselves, but dysreasoning effects prevent them from understanding this clearly (Ellis and Velten, 1992; Beck, Wright, Newman and Liese, 1993). "Stages of Change," as described by James Prochaska and colleagues, provides a framework for helping these people (Miller and Rollnick, 1991; Prochaska, Norcross, DiClemente, 1994). Their theory states that people move up and down through various stages while making changes in their lives. They describe the states as: Precontemplative, Contemplative, Preparation, Action, Maintenance and Termination (Prochaska, Norcross and DiClemente, 1994).

Prochaska and colleagues state that specific and different techniques are best employed for each stage. Conversely, applying the wrong technique in the wrong stage cannot only be ineffective, but can be counter-productive. For example, trying to teach someone the skills to solve a problem when they do not think they have a problem, is usually unproductive. Changes are more likely to occur when a person is receiving assistance formulated to match their current stage.

At the bottom of the "Stages of Change" are the Precontemplators. They are people who are not considering changing. They consist of people with three different outlooks regarding their AOD use.

One subgroup of Precontemplators consists of people who want to keep on drinking, but somehow avoid the negative consequences it brings upon them (Ellis, McInerney, DiGiuseppe and Yeager, 1988). Often their thinking concerning AOD is irrational and naive. They do not tell themselves that they are contributing to their own problems, but rather blame someone or something else. They are likely to consider the need for change when they begin to seriously think about what they gain from drinking and what it costs them. If they conclude that it may be costing them more than they realized, they will become curious and be interested in learning more.

The second group of Precontemplators consists of people who at one point in their lives tried to control their drinking and reduce their problems, but failed and have given up trying to change. They often have irrational ideas about their inability to direct their own lives. They feel hopeless and see themselves as powerless. They will remain in this stage until their beliefs are refuted and their confidence in their own ability is restore.

The third group, the "never-habilitated," consists of people whose whole lives have been so chaotic, deprived or painful that they cannot envision a clear reason to cut back or quit. In fact, drinking may be one of the few sources of good feelings they can consistently count on. They are the least likely to see the need for self-change. They do consider changing, however, if they discover that there are many things in this world that are worth having and that it is possible to obtain them.

In the Contemplative stage, people begin to weigh more thoroughly the pros and cons of their AOD use. They progress most when they find information about what their AOD use is doing to them. Contemplators who decided that their drinking is costing them more than it is worth, may decide to make some changes and move on to the Preparation stage.

In the Preparation stage, people begin to explore the various methods for changing: addiction counseling, AA, NA, Christ-Based 12-steps, Rational Recovery, Smart Recovery, Secular Organization for Sobriety, Women for Sobriety, Moderation Management, medications like Naltrexone and just quitting or cutting back on one's own, to name a few.

In the Action stage, a person has made a personal commitment to change. They put their plan into action. During the Maintenance stage, their new behaviors are becoming habits and their focus turns to learning ways to deal effectively with those life problems that are making it difficult to maintain their program (Ellis, McInerney, DiGiuseppe and Yeager, 1988).

Termination is the point where a person's aspirations have been readjusted. They have soundly established new methods for dealing with any remaining urges to use that are inconsistent with their better judgment. They have successfully cut back or quit. Termination does not mean a person necessarily stops their program. That depends on the individual and the program. However, they can easily dismiss any remaining cravings without discomfort.

C. Motivational Enhancement

The motivational enhancement approaches seek to guide PAOD users primarily through the Precontemplation and Contemplation stages. Motivational Interviewing, as expounded by William Miller and Stephan Rollnick, uses a non-confrontational approach to help PAOD users clarify their aspirations and move them towards less problematic behavior (1991). It is an empathic client-centered approach to counseling, but uses specific techniques that direct a person toward reducing their ambivalence in favor of a stable and a more self-enhancing life style.

D. Cognitive Therapy

Cognitive therapy helps PAOD users see that their behavior is self-defeating by having them explore their lives, beliefs and values and discovering what beliefs need to be changed in order for them to get what they want (Ellis, McInerney, DiGiuseppe and Yeager, 1988; Beck, Wright, Newman and Liese, 1993).

E. Abstinence/Moderation

One of the first major decision is whether an individual should abstain or learn to moderate. While this remains a controversial topic in the United States, it is less so elsewhere (Cameron, 1995). As stated earlier, illegal drugs always run the risk of being self-defeating. Teaching moderation skills for illegal drug use presents some interesting ethical questions.

Users on the less problematic end of the continuum probably do not need to be abstinent in order to end their problems. Nor will they likely comply with the drastic prescriptions that often come with abstinence-based treatments. Instead, many will either avoid treatment altogether or drop out, rather than learning any new knowledge or skills. They will just muddle-through and their behavior remain problematic.

Ellis and colleagues suggest that moderation training might be appropriate for those who (1988, p. 15):

> a) are not highly physically dependant on alcohol, b) do not have a long history of frequent alcohol-related problems, and c) are attainably flexible enough to work hard at reasserting some degree of control over their alcohol use.

Moderation management is a self-help group that promotes moderation as a means of ending problematic alcohol use (Kishline, 1994). They acknowledge that their program is not suitable for all problematic alcohol users. They do not recommend that anyone abandon abstinence if they have already found it to be a solution to their problems. However, they provide a program that outlines how to limit one's drinking. They further recommend that if an individual cannot maintain their program, that abstinence is likely the only solution.

Not only is this consistent with the PAOD continuum perspective, it is the advise of Alcoholics Anonymous. "If anyone who is showing inability to control his drinking can do the right-about-face and drink like a gentleman, our hats are off to him" (AA, 2001, p. 31).

If a person is at the most problematic end of the PAOD continuum, if moderation training fails or even moderation is successful but requires too great an effort to maintain, abstinence is probably the most viable strategy.

F. Dealing with Cravings

With either moderation or abstinence, dealing with cravings is a primary task. The first step is to recognize the thoughts that urge one to use (Ellis, McInerney, DiGiuseppe and Yeager, 1988).

Boy, that cheesecake would taste good. I love cherry cheesecake. But I shouldn't. It's not good for me. Besides, I promised myself I would stop overeating. If I eat too much of that stuff I'll have a heart attack. But it isn't that big of a piece. That little piece wouldn't make that big of a difference. It would really taste good. Cheesecake isn't that bad. Other people eat fried foods all the time. That's worse. They never get sick. I don't do that bad. Still there are a lot of calories in cheesecake. I used to be pretty fit. Look at me now. I can't get into my old cloths anymore. What difference does it make? I diet and diet and I never lose anything for long. I'll never get back to what I used to be. Besides, as you get older you're supposed to gain weight. What's the use of trying? I work hard and don't get much pleasure in life. I deserve a piece of cheesecake once in a while. And look at my doctor. He's fat. I'm not fat, I'm just a little over weight. I bet he eats cheesecake all the time and worse. I bet worse. To hell with it. I'm just going to eat it.

Just like with the cheesecake, there are emotionally biased thoughts that urge a person to drink in spite of their better judgment. Rational Recovery provides the following examples of such emotionally biased drinking thoughts (Trimpey, 1996, p.116):

1. Screw it. Just do it.
2. It can't really be any different.
3. I am an alcoholic, and that's why I drink.
4. I want it, so I'll have some. To hell with it.
5. I'll be careful this time. Just a little won't hurt.
6. You've been good for five days now. You deserve a drink.
7. I haven't had anything for two weeks, and I still feel lousy. A drink will help me feel better. Sobriety sucks, anyhow.
8. Life sucks. There is only one thing that feels right. A drink.

9. I feel good. A drink will make this a perfect moment.
10. I'm in good health. My body can take it.
11. I'm in bad health. What's the use of quitting?
12. I *need* alcohol to regulate my body. My body *requires* it.
13. What will people think if I don't drink? They may think I have a drinking problem.
14. I can't stand this constant craving. I may as well get it over with and drink.
15. I can't go more than (three days, one month, etc.) without drinking. It's time to drink again.
16. Drinking enriches my life. It's one of life's few genuine pleasures.
17. I can't stand feeling so bored (stressed, depressed, anxious, angry, etc.). I need a drink right now.
18. This is a very special occasion. It wouldn't be right without having a drink.
19. I can't enjoy music, TV, food, parties, sex, traveling, or have fun without drinking.
20. I need something to relax after a hard day's work.

Drinking in spite of persistent negative consequences is an indication that a person's emotionally based thoughts are producing cravings, while their better judgment is being blocked by dysreasoning effects. Part of ending one's PAOD is becoming aware of any emotionally biased thoughts that support drinking in problematic ways. Another need is to effectively control dysreasoning effects.

The second step in dealing with cravings is to not challenge or debate the thoughts that urge one to drink. Doing so actually creates an obsession-like condition (Wegner, 1990). For example, try not to think of a white bear. Do you find that difficult? You might have thoughts similar to: *Now I shouldn't think about a white bear. Oh no! I just thought about a white bear. Darn. I just did it again. When I try not to think about a white bear, I think about one.*

Trying to not think about something can make you think about it (Wegner, 1990). If you are trying to resist cravings by not thinking about drinking, you inadvertently remind yourself to think about it. Following Wilde's advice, one should not resist the drinking thoughts, debate them or dispute them. However, contrary to his advice, a person should not yield to them. A person should just acknowledge the drinking thoughts and keep on doing whatever it is that they are doing when the cravings intruded into their mind. They should absorb themselves with the activity at hand (Wegner, 1990).

If a person consistently does not act on thoughts that urge a particular behavior, their brain eventually rewires itself. The neurological paths laid down by new thoughts and activities are reinforced, while the neurological paths laid down by the old thoughts and activities are extinguishing (Schwartz, 2002). This applies to AOD use as well as to most other behaviors.

On a biological level, these changes occur because of the brain's neuroplasticity. This refers to the "ability of neurons to forge new connections, to blaze new paths through the cortex, even to assume new roles" (Schwartz, 2002, p. 15). What you pay attention to literally changes the physical structure and functioning of the brain.

The primary cognitive skill for dealing with cravings is similar to Dr. Jeffrey Schwartz's treatment for Obsessive-Compulsive Disorder (1996, 2002):

> Step 1: Relabel: Recognize obsessive thoughts and compulsive urges with mindful awareness: *This thought is an obsession; this urge is a compulsive urge.*
>
> Step 2: Reattribute: Remind yourself that the obsessive thought and compulsive urge is not meaningful, that they are false messages from the brain. *It's not me—it's my OCD.*
>
> Step 3: Refocus: With OCD part of the brain, the caudate nucleus is stuck. It makes the sufferer feel that an import task is not complete and that bad things will happen unless the task is completed. But with OCD that feeling of completion never comes - thus the repetitive behavior. With refocusing, the OCD sufferer shifts their mind manually. They work around the false messages by keeping their attention on something else – doing another behavior, any pleasant, constructive behavior. The objective is not to feel good, but rather to control the behavior until the OCD feelings wane and fade.

Step 4: Revalue: Eventually, though persistent working around the false messages, the brain changes, the obsessions and compulsions weaken and can easily be dismissed without discomfort.

Schwartz's steps can be adapted to deal with AOD cravings as follows:

Step 1: Recognize: Recognize that any thought, image or feeling that urges you to use is your user's voice. *That's my user's voice that wants me to drink.*

Step 2: Separate: Remind yourself that you no longer choose to use. *My user's voice wants a drink. I do not drink.*

Step 3: Carry On: Keep your mind from shifting attention to your user's voice by going about your business. Do not try to not think about the user's voice, but rather just keep your mind on life's everyday tasks. You cannot be mindful of doing something and think of drinking at the same time. At first, the user's voice will intrude and make you feel uncomfortable. However, the objective is not to feel good, but rather to keep busy until the bad feelings wane and fade.

Step 4: Reconfigure: Eventually, through persistently working around the drinking thoughts, your brain will reconfigure itself and your user's voice will weaken and fade away. At that point, you will be able to easily dismiss it without distress.

G. Other Concerns

Besides dealing with cravings, other tasks will need to be addressed depending on the person's drinking profile and program. If a person is using to escape withdrawal effects, they will need to go through detoxification. If they had been a recreational/social user, they will need to find other sources of recreations and new friends. If they were drinking to escape bad feelings, they will need to resolve the problems that are causing them distress and learn the skills to keep new problems from developing, especially those dealing with negative emotions, interpersonal conflict and social pressures to drink (Parks and Marlatt, 2000).

While a person cannot undo their genetic predispositions, new drugs are being developed that can help counteract the effects of AOD use (Neuroscience Research and

Medication Development, 1996). For example, alcohol's intoxicating effect is blocked when a person takes Naltrexone. They can then work on the other factors that are contributing to their PAOD without intoxication complicating matters.

Finally, a person learned to use alcohol and other drugs in a variety of social setting and for a variety of social purposes. If a person is to successfully end their problems, it is helpful to avoid these situations (or at least be prepared for them) until they are in the Maintenance stage and have learned new strategies for engaging in those situation that do not involve the use of alcohol or other drugs (Ellis, McInerney, DiGiuseppe and Yeager, 1988; Parks and Marlatt, 2000).

XI. SUMMARY AND CONCLUSION

Alcohol and other drug use exists on a continuum with extremely problematic behavior on one end and non-problematic behavior on the other. The biopsychosocial factors that make AOD use attractive will determine a person's place on the continuum and the character of their drinking or using behavior The more factors, the greater their magnitudes and the greater their variety, the more attractive AOD use becomes. High levels of attraction result in high levels of ambivalence and resistance to changing drinking or using habits in the face of problems. Discovering the specific factors that contribute to a person's attraction to AOD and their inability to change in the face of persistent problems will help direct the specific strategies needed to end or reduce their PAOD. Anything less is inadequate.

The cognitive-behavioral psychology explained in this paper describes how a person's decisions can become emotionally biased in favor of drinking and using in spite of persistent problems. The same psychology also offers a foundation on which interventions can be fashioned to reduce or eliminate problematic emotionally biased thoughts and behaviors. Those interventions would take the form of value clarification, cognitive restructuring, refuting irrational beliefs, reality therapy, recognizing risky situations, behavioral rehearsals, management of emotions, relaxation training and problem solving.

Cognitive-behavioral therapies have been shown to be one of the most effective approaches for treating "alcoholic" patients (Longabaugh and Morgenstern, 1999). Most of these therapies do not focus on alcohol consumption issues, but rather "address other life areas that often are functionally related to drinking and relapse" (Longabaugh and Morgenstern, 1999). This corresponds to providing non-AOD alternatives for the recreational/social and palliative psychological relief reward types.

Traditional PAOD cognitive-behavioral techniques are less effective when used as stand-alone treatment (Longabaugh and Morgenstern, 1999). This might be do to the fact they do not provided methods for dealing with cravings and urges to drink or to escape withdrawal effects. The psychology described in this paper provides an additional technique for dealing with cravings and ambivalence in the modification of Schwartz's treatment for Obsessive-Compulsive Disorder (1996, 2002). This might provided a new tool to add to the PAOD cognitive-behavioral arsenal.

XII. AFTERWORD

Many years ago, as a young probation officer, I visited the home a young man indicated he planned to live in once paroled from prison. He had a terrible drinking problem and had been to prison twice before. As I talked to his wife, a school bus dropped a little girl off. She was maybe seven or eight.

She came in and stood beside me. I smiled at her and said hello. She did not respond. She just stood there and stared at me. I thought she might be shy around strangers and did not give it a second thought. After a couple of minutes, I felt a tug on my shirt. I turned to look at the little girl and she asked me, *Are you my daddy?* Even after nearly thirty years, I cannot think of this without feeling very sad.

Problematic alcohol and drug use is a broad challenge requiring broad solutions. Current treatment perspectives generally address only a portion of the problem and few provide help for Precontemplators and Contemplators. Until our perspective is expanded to take into account all of the factors that contribute to a person's problematic use, there will continue to be many people left behind and more little girls who do not know their daddies.

Moral Justification: Bad behavior is excused by reframing it as a social or moral good. For example, *It's all right to do a little speed in order to think clear and work harder.*

Euphemistic Language: Bad behavior is made to feel less so by using language that minimizes the harm done. For example, *It is all right to sell drugs when your customers are just using them for fun.*

Advantageous Comparison: The belief of having done something wrong is minimized by comparing oneself with others who are doing worse things. For example, *I only drove after a few beers. It's not like I robbed a bank or something.*

Displacement of Responsibility: The belief of having done something wrong is minimized when it is viewed as has having a cause outside of your control. For example, *You can't blame me. I'm an alcoholic. I can't help myself.*

Diffusion of Responsibility: The belief of having done something wrong is minimized by spreading the blame among many other people. For example, *You can't blame me. Everyone else is doing it.*

Distorting Consequences: Harmful behavior is minimized by disregarding or reducing the belief about the harm done. For example, *No one was really hurt that much.*

Attribution of Blame: Bad behavior is dissipated when a person blames someone else for having given them no choice for their behavior. For example, *I wouldn't have gotten drunk him if she hadn't made me angry.*

Dehumanization: The belief of having done something wrong is dissipated if you see the victim as less than human. For example, *Straight people are so stupid. To hell with them.*

Adapted from
Albert Bandura

Bibliography:

Alcohol and cognition. (1989). *National Institute on Alcohol Abuse and Alcoholism, 4.* [Online] Available: http://www.niaaa.nih.gov/publications/aa04.htm. [2003, April 7].

Alcohol and minorities: An update. (2002). *National Institute on Alcohol Abuse and Alcoholism, 55,* [Online] Available: http://www.niaaa.nih.gov/publications/aa55.htm. [2003, October 28].

Alcohol and stress. (1996). *National Institute on Alcohol Abuse and Alcoholism, 32.* [Online] Available: http://www.niaaa.nih.gov/publications/aa32.htm. [2003, October 28].

Alcohol and tolerance. (1995). *National Institute on Alcohol Abuse and Alcoholism, 28,* [Online] Available: http://www.niaaa.nih.gov/publications/aa28.htm. [2003, April 7].

Alcoholics Anonymous. (2001) *Alcoholics Anonymous.* (4th ed.). New York: Alcoholics Anonymous World Service.

Alcohol-related impairment. (1994). *National Institute on Alcohol Abuse and Alcoholism, 25,* [Online] Available: http://www.niaaa.nih.gov/publications/aa25.htm. [2003, April 7].

Alcohol withdrawal syndrome. (1998). *National Institute on Alcohol Abuse and Alcoholism, 5,* [Online] Available: http://www.niaaa.nih.gov/publications/aa05.htm. [2003, April 7].

American Psychiatric Association (1994). *Diagnostic and statistical manual of mental disorders – DSM-IV.* Washington, DC: The American Psychiatric Association.

Andrews, D., Bonta, J. (1998). *The psychology of criminal conduct.* (2nd. ed.). Cincinnati: Anderson Publishing.

Arnsten, A. (1998). The biology of being frazzled, *Science, 280,* 1711-1712.

Bandura, A., Barbaranelli, C., Caprara, G. V., Pastorelli, C. (1996). Mechanisms of moral disengagement in the exercise of moral agency. *Journal of Personality and Social Psychology, 71,* 364-374.

Beck, A., Wright, F., Newman, C., Liese, B. (1993). *Cognitive therapy of substance abuse.* New York: Guilford Press.

Beck, J. (1995). *Cognitive therapy: Basics and beyond.* New York: Guilford Press.

Begley, T. (1998). Coping strategies as predictors of employee distress and turnover after an organizational consolidation: A longitudinal analysis. *Journal of Occupational and Organizational Psychology, 71,* 305-329.

Benson, N. (2001). *Introducing psychology.* Cambridge: Icon Books.

Blum, K., Cull, J., Braverman, E., Comings, D. (1996). Reward deficiency syndrome. *American Scientist, March-April 1996,* [Online] Available: http://www.americanscientist.org/articles/96articles/blum-full.html. [2002, August 17]

Burns, D. (1980). *Feeling good: The new mood therapy.* New York: Avon Books.

Cameron, D. (1995). *Liberating solution to alcohol problems: Treating problem drinkers without saying no.* London: Jason Aronson Inc.

Carroll, L. (1982). Through the looking glass and what Alice found there. In E. Guiliano (Ed.), *The complete illustrated works of Lewis Carroll* (pp. 81-176). New York: Avenel Books.

Chester, M. (1978). *Particles: An introduction to particle physics.* New York: Mentor.

Chiara, GC. (1977). Alcohol and dopamine. *Alcohol Health & Research World, 21:2,* 108-113.

Damasio, A. (1994). *Descartes' error: Emotion, reason, and the human brain.* New York: Avon Books.

Davis, M., Eshelman, E., McKay, M. (1988). *The relaxation & stress reduction workbook.* (3rd Ed.). Oakland, CA: New Harbinger Publications.

Ekman, P. (1992). An argument for basic emotions, *Cognition and Emotions, 6,* 169-200.

Ellis, A., Harper, R. (1961). *A guide to rational living.* Hollywood, CA: Wilshire Book Company.

Ellis, A., McInerney, J., DiGiuseppe, R., Yeager, R. (1988). *Rational-emotive therapy with alcohol and substance abusers.* Boston: Allyn and Bacon.

Ellis, A., Velten, E. (1992). *When AA doesn't work for you: Rational steps to quitting alcohol.* New York: Barricade Books.

Epstein, S., Brodsky, A. (1993). *You're smarter than you think: How to develop your practical intelligence for success in living.* New York: Simon & Schuster.

Epstein, S. (1994). Integration of the cognitive and psychodynamic unconscious. *American Psychologist, 49,* 709-724.

Epstein, S. (1998). *Constructive thinking: The key to emotional intelligence*. Westport, CT: Praeger.

Ewing, J. A. (1980). Alcoholism another biopsychosocial disease. *Psychosomatics, 21:5*, 371-372.

Festinger, L. (1957). *A theory of cognitive dissonance.* Stanford: Stanford University Press.

Fishman, R. (1986). *The encyclopedia of psychoactive drugs.* New York: Chelsea House.

Freeman, A., DeWolf, R. (1992). The 10 dumbest mistakes smart people make and how to avoid them. New York: HarperPerennial.

Gardner, R., Kemer, E. (1993). *Making and using scientific models.* New York: Franklin Watts.

Genetics of alcoholism. (1992). *National Institute on Alcohol Abuse and Alcoholism, 18.* [Online] Available: http://www.niaaa.nih.gov/publications/aa18.htm. [2003, October 28].

Goleman, D. (1995). *Emotional intelligence: Why it can matter more than IQ.* New York: Bantam Books.

Jones, R., Lacy, J. (2000). State of knowledge of alcohol-impaired driving: Research on repeat DWI offenders. *National Highway Traffic Safety Administration.* [On line] Available: Http://www.nhtsa.dot.gov/people/injury/research/pub/alcohol-im-paireddriving.html. [2003, August 19].

Keirsey, D. (1998). *Please understand me II: Temperament character intelligence.* Del Mar, CA.: Prometheus Nemesis.

Kishline, A. (1994) *Moderation drinking: The moderation management guide.* New York: Three Rivers Press.

Lazarus, R., Folkman, S. (1984). *Stress, appraisal and coping.* New York: Springer.

LeDoux, J. (1996). *The emotional brain: The mysterious underpinnings of emotional life.* New York: Touchstone.

LeDoux, J. (2002). *Synaptic self: How our brains become who we are.* New York: Viking.

Longabaugh, R., Morgenstern, J. (1999). Cognitive-behavioral coping-skills therapy for alcohol dependence. *Alcohol Research & Health, 23:21*, 78-85.

McCarthy, J. G., Stewart, A. L. (1998). Neutralisation as a process of graduated desensitisation: Moral values of offenders. *International Journal of Offender Therapy and Comparative Criminology, 42*, 278-290.

McGuire, M., Troisi, A. (1998). *Darwinian psychiatry.* New York: Oxford University Press.

Miller, W., Rollnick, S. (1991). *Motivational Interviewing: Preparing people to change addictive behavior.* New York: Gilford Press.

Moore, D. (2001). *The dependent gene.* New York: time Books.

Myers, D. (2002). *Intuition: Its powers and perils.* New Haven: Yale University Press.

National Highway Transportation Safety Administration. (1996). *A guide to sentencing DUI offenders.* Report No. DOT HS 808 365.

National Institute of Health. (1998). *Drinking in the United States: Main findings from the 1992 National Longitudinal Alcohol Epidemiologic Survey (NLAES).* NHI Publication No. 99-3519.

Nature's own antidote to cocaine: Brain opiate may explain why some people are less susceptible to addiction. [Online]. Available: http://eurekalert.org/pub_releases/2002-04/ru-noa041202.php. [2002, April 16].

Nestler, E. (2002). The genetic basis of addiction. *Psychiatric Times, XIX, 2.* [Online] Available: http://www.psychiatrictimes.com/p020256.html. [2003, October 28].

Neuroscience research and medication development. (1996). *National Institute on Alcohol Abuse and Alcoholism, 33.* [Online] Available: http://www.niaaa.nih.gov/publications/aa33.htm. [2003, September 19].

Parks, G., Marlatt, G. (2000). Relapse prevention therapy: A cognitive-behavioral approach. *The National Psychologist.* [Online] Available: http://www.nationalpsychologist.com/articles/art_v9n5_3htm. [2003, September 20].

Pilgrim. D. (2003). The biopsychosocial model in Anglo-American psychiatry: Past, present and future. [Online]. Available: http://www.critpsynet.freeuk.com/Pilgrim.htm. [2003, April 22].

Pinker, S. (1997). *How the mind works.* New York: W. W. Norton and Co.

Prochaska, J., Norcross, J., DiClemente, C. (1994). *Changing for good.* New York: William Morrow and company.

Relapse and cravings. (1989) *National Institute on Alcohol Abuse and Alcoholism, 6,* [Online] Available: http://www.niaaa.nil.gov/publications/aa06.htm. [2003, April 7].

Ridley, M. (2003). *Nature via nurture: Genes, experiences, & what makes us human.* New York: HarperCollins

Saitz, R. (1998). Introduction to alcohol withdrawal. *Alcohol health & Research World,* 22. 5-12.

Savage-Rumbaugh, S., Lewin, R. (1994). *Kanzi: The ape at the brink of the human mind.* Indianapolis: Wiley.

Schwartz, J. (1996). *Brain lock: Free yourself from obsessive-compulsive behavior.* New York: ReganBooks

Schwartz, J. (2002). *The mind and the brain: Neuroplasticity and the power of mental force.* New York: ReganBooks.

Seligman, M. (1993). *What you can change and what you can't: The complete guide to successful self-improvement.* New York: Fawcett Columbine.

Tice, M., Bratslavsky, E., Baumeister, R. (2001) Emotional distress regulation takes precedence over impulse control: If you feel bad, do it. *Journal of Personality and Social Psychology, 80,* 53-67.

Tiffany, S. (1999). Cognitive concepts of craving. *Alcohol Health & Research World, 23:3,* 215-224.

Trimpey, J. (1996). *Rational recovery: The new cure for substance addiction.* New York: Pocket Books.

Toffler, A. (1970). *Future shock.* New York: Bantan Books

Wegner, D. (1990). *White bears & other unwanted thoughts: Suppression, obsession and the psychology.* New York: Penguin Books.

Wieczorek, F., Hansen, C. (1997) New modeling Methods: Geographic information systems and spatial analysis. *Alcohol, Health & Research World, 21:4,* 331-339.

Wilde, O. (1995). The Picture of Dorian Gray. In, *The picture of Dorian Gray and other stories* (pp.1-241). New York: Barnes & Noble.